MANN ABL.

A history of the Isle of Man Fire Service

BY STAN BASNETT

 in association with

MANN ABLAZE!

A history of the Isle of Man Fire Service

Published by Leading Edge Press & Publishing Ltd, in association with the Fire Brigade Society.

Leading Edge, The Old Chapel, Burtersett, Hawes,
North Yorkshire DL8 3PB
☎ (0969) 667566

British Library Cataloguing in Publication Data

Basnett, Stan, 1938-
    Mann Ablaze!
    1. Isle of Man. Fire-fighting, history.
    I. Title
    628.925094279

    ISBN 0-948135-25-5

Photographs: Stan Basnett (except where otherwise credited)
Type: Leading Edge Press & Publishing Ltd
Design: Stan Abbott
Printed and bound in Great Britain by Ebenezer Baylis and Son Ltd, Worcester

COVER PICTURES
Front: Fire at the demolition site of the Regal Cinema, Douglas, Easter 1984.
Back: The Summerland fire. Picture by Dave Wood.

Contents

Fire-fighting equipment in the days between the wars can appear rather rudimentary to modern eyes: this is the Laxey Village Commissioners' handcart of 1921.

Preface

THE PREFACE to a book was something I never used to read. Then, a little later, I would read it after I had completed the book. Now it is the first thing I look at.

I'm glad you have found the time to read my preface, as it is really the only chance that reader and writer have to get to know one another.

The desire to write a documentary history on one of the several subjects which interest me has been with me for many years. I have helped many of my friends to research books, and, through my interest in photography, I have made more friends by providing photographs to illustrate their work.

Why the fire service? Why the Isle of Man? The answer to the first is very involved, but suffice to say that my interest started with a course in fire prevention in my teens and stayed with me through my professional training to the point where, at one stage, I wanted to become a fire assessor. The answer to the second part is simple. As a Manxman, I believe that any documentary of our way of life will broaden the foundation of our heritage.

While the book deals with the development of the fire service within the Island, it also parallels such development in many rural areas of England, and I hope it will appeal to those outside the Island who are interested in the history of fire-fighting.

The development of the service has, quite properly, been founded on experience and I have tried to show how incidents have occurred which have led to legislation being passed in an effort to prevent their re-occurrence. In some instances, fires have highlighted the inadequacy of the equipment available and this, in turn, has led to the expansion of the service and the continuous updating of equipment.

This is the theme of the book: to a large extent it is chronological, although I have tried to avoid it becoming too much a list of facts and figures.

Throughout my research, two truths come to the fore: fire has nearly always been started by the careless use of the naked flame; and death at fires is usually the result of suffocation.

Research is a most peculiar pastime, as anyone who has delved into archives will admit. While researching the history of the Douglas brigade, I found that my great grandfather, Claude Cannell, had been elected to the Town Commissioners in 1866, and this fact was confirmed by my mother, who told me that she shared her Christian name, Janetta, with Mrs Cannell, née McGhie. "Not by any chance the daughter of the brassfounder in Parade Street?" I asked. "Yes, John McGhie," she affirmed, as if I should have known without asking.

So John McGhie, the mastermind behind the first fire engine owned by Douglas Council, was my great, great grandfather. Perhaps that is where my interest started. Who knows?

Stan Basnett, Glen Vine, May 1991

This photograph shows 12 of the 13 men who comprised what was almost certainly the first fire brigade to be formed in Ramsey, in 1887. Also depicted are examples of the type of equipment in use at that time, such as standpipes and long branches. Such branches, from the Castletown brigade, can be seen today in the Manx Museum, Douglas.

1. The beginnings

The arrival of the first fire engines on the Isle of Man

THE STORY of the Isle of Man Fire Service begins on Thursday, October 20, 1803, with the arrival of two fire engines by packet boat from Liverpool. They belonged to the Sun Fire Insurance office and were immediately taken into the care of its Douglas agent, James Moore. However, any history of the service must look at events in the preceding decades.

By 1707, legislation in England had placed a duty on the churchwardens of every parish to provide, maintain and repair a fire engine and other appliances. There was also a clear duty to provide fire plugs and a requirement for adjoining houses to have brick party walls. But there was no such legislation on the Isle of Man.

Official records of the workings of the Manx Government were introduced by Sir John de Stanley soon after he obtained the patent of Henry IV which vested control of the Island in Stanley and his heirs. The Manx Statute Book, dating from 1417, records that the High Bailiffs Act of 1777 introduced legislation which gave the Lieutenant Governor authority to appoint "...High Bailiffs for Castletown, Douglas, Peeltown and Ramsay (sic)...". The Act was intended to regulate the interior police of the Island and assist in the recovery of small debts. It also included a duty for the repair of streets and improvement of sanitary conditions in the various towns. The High Bailiffs were the administrators of the towns and they were soon to become involved in fighting outbreaks of fire.

In 1791, Sir Wadsworth Burke, the Attorney General, who lived at Newtown, in Santon, wrote: "Till the commencement of the present century, the people appear to have been extremely illiterate and ignorant, incapable of forming, or comprehending an abstract scheme of, civil government." It is against this con-temporary description of the people of the Island that we start to see how they began to protect life and property from fire.

The fear of fire spreading was the prime consideration at this time; the saving of life was of secondary importance. Properties were built very close together, separated by narrow streets and common courtyards. An unchecked fire in one property could quickly spread and engulf a whole street.

The Island was fortunate because most of its buildings were made of stone, although straw thatch was more common than slate as a roof covering. Properties were remote in the country districts; if fire broke out the occupants had either to watch it burn or rely on limited supplies of water from wells or streams and, occasionally, help from neighbours.

Townsfolk were in a better position, as there were more people ready to fight a fire — if only to stop it spreading to their own properties.

The earliest records of watching appear in the orders and duties of the soldiers at Castle Rushen and Peel Castle, which stated that "the night bell be rung a little after sun setting and that by the porter, and the constable with his deputie, with a sufficient guard, be in the castle for the safe keeping and defence of the same". Further, the porter was instructed to go about the walls and see that all was clear and that "every soldier, at the sound of the drum or ringing of the Allarum Bell, shall forthwith make his presence at the gate". Clearly, these men were disciplined, ready to meet any contingency, including fire, as is apparent in some of the early reports of fires.

There were barracks in Douglas in the early part of the 19th century and the same garrison orders applied. On Saturday, August 20, 1803, the miller at the Nunnery Mill, just outside

Douglas, left work and closed the door behind him. He did not know that barley, left to dry on the second floor, had begun to smoulder. The heat in the store built up overnight; at 8.30am on Sunday fire broke out.

The miller sent a lad into town to raise the alarm. A number of active people soon assembled at the mill and managed to extinguish the blaze in two hours.

Contemporary reports do not specifically mention the militia's presence at this fire, but they do record that the fire engines had not yet arrived on the Island, having been detained at Liverpool by the Sun Fire Office for want of mechanics to complete their assembly.

Since 1801 the Sun Fire Office had been offering insurance in the Island, through its Douglas agent, at the rate of four shillings (20 pence) for every hundred pounds insured. It was through the demands of local subscribers that pressure was brought to bear on the Sun Fire Office in London; two fire engines were sent to the Island a couple of years later.

There was still no organised fire brigade and the local agent relied on volunteers to man the engines whenever they were called out. People living in the out-of-town areas were still no better off, because of the time required to send word to Douglas and then drag the engine to the scene of the fire.

Trouble at mills

The need for those outside Douglas to fend for themselves is well illustrated by events surrounding a fire at the mining village of Laxey, six miles north of Douglas, on Saturday, May 9, 1804, when Brockbank's spinning mill caught light. Miners in a nearby pub quickly organised a bucket chain and managed to put the flames out before they reached the machines, though most of the stock was damaged.

The fire had been started, it was discovered, by a young employee playing with a candle.

Bakehouses and mills presented a high fire risk through the very nature of their business. In February 1805 such a fire occurred in Oates' Lane, Douglas, when an oven flue overheated and set fire to the thatch. The *Manx Advertiser* reported that "...although considerable alarm was at first created in the neighbourhood, we are happy to add that the fire was extinguished without doing more than unroofing the Bakehouse".

Two years later another fire broke out in a bakehouse, again setting fire to the thatch. This time there was considerable panic as a large quantity of gunpowder was kept in the ordnance storehouse nearby. The fire engine was brought and operated by the crowd while the militia moved the gunpowder. James Moore directed the helpers and got the fire under control, but not before the building was gutted and adjoining properties damaged. It was fortunate that the fire happened in the daytime; a fire at night would have proved disastrous.

Fire broke out again in the drying kiln at the Nunnery Mill on Friday, April 1, 1808. Mr Hastings, the miller, discovered the blaze at about 2am and sent to Douglas for help. The alarm was raised by ringing the chapel bell and sounding the drum at the barracks. Soldiers and townsfolk took two engines to the mill; they prevented fire from spreading throughout the building, although the kiln was gutted and grain stocks damaged. Men were still there in the afternoon removing smouldering grain, and they were rewarded for their efforts by two barrels of ale.

It is difficult to be certain of events which happened so long ago, but it would seem that one of the two engines which arrived at Douglas in 1803 was sent to Ramsey. The minutes of the management committee of the Sun Fire Office in London record that five guineas were spent on repairs to the engine at Ramsey in February 1806. Yet by 1808 both engines were back in Douglas.

These early engines were normally drawn by hand and could take water from a stream or pond. If such a supply was unavailable, the body of the engine — which acted as a cistern — could be filled from leather buckets passed by hand. The larger of the two engines at Douglas could be drawn by horse if required. The pump needed between 16 and 20 men to operate it.

Not everybody was insured against fire, but this did not limit the use of the engine. Mr Leeson, a draper living above his premises in Lord Street, found this out to his cost, when, at 7pm on Wednesday, December 27, 1815, a servant's candle set fire to his bedroom curtains. The fire soon took a firm hold.

On the first alarm, the chapel bell was rung, the drum beat to arms and a detachment of the Manx Volunteer Infantry was despatched from the barracks. The fire engine was soon on the spot and "many gentlemen of respectability were actively employed in bringing water to the engine".

There was no mains water supply at this time; water had to be passed by leather bucket from the nearest well or other source. The Douglas Waterworks Act, which was to give the necessary power for the provision of a piped water supply, was not introduced until 1834.

The fire was fierce and threatened adjoining property. Mr Leeson's neighbours helped to remove most of his valuable stock, but his living accommodation was completely gutted by the time the fire was put out. Mr Leeson had insured the building, but the policy had lapsed.

During this period it was a common occurance for candles to set fire to curtains and bed-drapes. For all but the very wealthy, a candle was the only source of light.

A similar fire occurred in January 1832 at Knockan House, a country farm belonging to a Mr Thompson. Mr Richmond and his family, friends of the Thompsons, were staying at Knockan House and, on New Year's Day, Mrs Richmond gave birth to twins. Three days later, Mrs Thompson was reading a letter to her by candlelight. The flame caught the flutings of the bed curtains, which were instantly ablaze. Mrs Richmond leapt from the bed; she and the nurse carried the twins downstairs, while Mrs Thompson tried to beat out the flames with pillows.

Mr Thompson, some distance away at the stables, rushed to the house and, with Mr Richmond and some farm labourers, organised a bucket chain from the pump in the yard.

Fortunately the fire was out very quickly, but Mr Thompson's plight was typical of many in country districts: help was too far away to be of any use. If you were not quick and resourceful, there was little alternative but to stand and watch your property burn. Mr Thompson was also prudent in being insured by the Norwich Fire Office.

A fire of a different kind occurred in Douglas the following year. It was to test the town's fire-fighting resources to the limit; had it not been extinguished quickly, or at least contained, then a large part of the town would surely have been engulfed.

The harbour was the heart of Douglas. Many merchants had fine homes fronting onto it, with warehouses close by and the houses of the town huddled tightly behind.

A bakehouse owned by a Mr T Kinrade and a joiner's shop occupied by Mr N Moore adjoined one another in Queen Street, which led off the quay. These properties backed on to Mr W Stephen's property on the North Quay. At the other end, a narrow yard separated them from Forbes's warehouse, stocked with grain, tallow and spirits, and houses belonging to Mrs Dumbell and Mr Curphey.

On Sunday, March 24, 1833, at 7pm, someone in Mr Curphey's house saw flames coming from the roof of the joiner's shop. The flames, fanned by a strong north-east breeze, soon embraced the bakehouse.

The alarm was raised and messengers sent for the Sun Insurance Company's engines. They were quickly on the spot, but flames were already beating against the adjoining houses and burning embers were being carried over the town by the wind.

His Honour Deemster Heywood was one of the first to arrive. He took charge, issuing instructions to the men working the engines, and Messrs Moore and Clarke of the Sun Office organised water carts between the harbour and the engines. A good water supply was obtained, despite it being nearly low water.

Word spread rapidly through the town and into the various places of worship. Such was the panic that people were jammed in the doors of St Barnabas' Chapel, as they rushed to see if their properties were affected.

It was soon apparent that nothing could be done to save the bakehouse and joiner's shop, so efforts were made to stop the fire spreading. Household furniture and personal belongings were removed from adjacent houses, but some of the several hundred onlookers were less than honest. The Chief Constable had a hard job to control them and stop them hindering the progress of the water carts.

At 8.30pm the roof fell in and the firemen were able to gain better control of the blaze. Shortly after 9pm, the fire, which had been leaping across the yard by Forbes's warehouse, set light to a wooden downspout which in turn kindled the roof. Efforts were quickly directed on to it and by 9.30pm it was put out. Shortly afterwards the gutted remains of the bakehouse were damped down and the fire finally extinguished. Small fires on the roofs of nearby properties, started by flying embers, were put out by patrols carrying water buckets. Douglas had had a close call.

The fire was presumed to have been caused by sparks and burning soot falling from the flue of the bakehouse into the flue of the joiner's shop. Both were in the same stack and, in the manner of the period, separated by timber boards or "midfeathers". The sparks ignited sawdust on the floor of the joiner's shop, which smouldered for some time before setting fire to the roof.

Out in the country

The following year, a number of country fires occurred where no help was available. In March, Gelling and Moore's new corn mill at Cregwillysill was completely destroyed by a fire which started in the drying kiln. June saw a serious fire at Ballakissack, in Santon, where the farmhouse was destroyed after bed hangings caught fire. The next month, neighbours returning home from Arbory Fair found one of the houses at Ronague on fire and, with some difficulty, raised the inmates. Despite the number of people on the scene, the fire spread quickly to the thatched roof and then to the neighbouring house; both properties were gutted.

Thatched roofs were clearly a high fire risk, a risk made greater by the isolation of country properties. A woman by the name of Crellin, who lived in Ballaugh, left her son in the house while she went into the yard to pound gorse, used for dyeing wool. Unsupervised, the boy put more fuel—also gorse—on the fire. It flared, set fire to more gorse stacked in the hearth, and within minutes had spread to the thatched roof. The cottage was reduced to four bare walls.

On Sunday, January 14, 1844, another fire—at King William's College, the well-known school on the outskirts of Castletown—

further illustrated the problems facing isolated country districts. The fire started in the dining hall of the Principal's house. It was discovered at 3.30am, and immediate steps were taken to rescue the boys in the dormitory. But so fierce was the fire that the flames spread rapidly up the staircase, forcing some to retreat and escape by a communicating attic door through the Vice-principal's house.

The fire was spotted from Castle Rushen, about a mile and a half away, by the sentinel on guard duty. A detachment of the Sixth (the King's) Liverpool Regiment turned out in double quick time under the command of Captain Griffith and Lieutenant Staunton. They were almost the first on the scene and rendered prompt assistance in saving college property from the flames. A roll call was taken and everyone was accounted for. Masters and boys then set about preventing the spread of fire by packing wet blankets at the doors and removing the intervening roof.

Expert help was needed so the captain sent a courier to Douglas on horseback to summon the engines of the Sun Fire Office. The Governor of the Island was soon on the scene; he directed attempts to halt the fire which was being fanned by a north-westerly gale. But it was to no avail. At 6am flames broke through the west door of the chapel and engulfed it. Half an hour later the whole of the college, except the Vice-principal's house, was on fire and flames reached 125ft up the central tower.

Once word had reached Douglas, the engines immediately set off. However, because of slippery roads they did not arrive at the school until 9am — five hours after the courier had left Castletown.

The wind died down, enabling workmen to block up communicating doors between the schoolrooms. This, together with the efforts of the firemen, enabled the fire to be contained and eventually extinguished.

Once again the main problem facing the fire-fighters was an inadequate water supply, a well being the only source. The nearest fire-fighting appliances were at Douglas, a fact which highlighted the need for improved communication between the towns and the provision of more equipment.

The college lost an irreplaceable library of books given by its founder, Bishop Wilson, together with most of its buildings. Damage amounted to £4,000, but it was insured for only £2,000 with the Sun Fire Office.

The fire was a sobering experience for all who witnessed it. The incident also reflected badly on Castletown which was, after all, the seat of government and capital of the Island. The matter was discussed between the Governor and the militia; in 1845 the garrison took delivery of a fire engine built by J Stone, of Deptford.

Two years later, in Douglas, concern was being expressed at the inadequacy of the insurance engines in the event of fire in the town; this was at a time when communications between the towns were improving. Coaches left the market place every day for Castletown and Peel; the public could travel in the *John Bull* or the *Falcon* and return the same day. The coaches *Prince of Wales* and *Regulator* left Douglas on alternate days for Ramsey and returned the following day.

The year 1847 was particularly bad for mill fires. The worst one was at Peel: the windmill at Ballaquane was completely destroyed, there being no fire engine in the area.

In June a fire broke out in Mr Stowell's druggist's shop at Castletown. A young shop assistant was sent with a young girl to the cellar to get some oil. He took a candle but, being inquisitive, stopped to look in the bottles stored there. He opened a bottle of naphtha, which ignited from the candle flame. Both were injured.

Fire immediately spread and clouds of black smoke filled the shop and the house. Mr Stowell's sister was on the third floor of the house and, on hearing the commotion, she panicked and tried to jump out of the window. A man ran through the smoke and rescued her. The boy and girl were dragged from the cellar and the alarm was raised at the Barracks.

The garrison engine was soon on the spot. The floor was broken by the officer directing the soldiers, who played the hose through it and onto the fire. The engine was worked by the soldiers and, with the assistance of the inhabitants of the town, a bucket chain was formed between a public pump and the engine.

The fire was eventually put out, but damage was considerable and adjoining shops had been endangered.

At 2am on Tuesday, September 27 the following year, a fierce fire was discovered in the Fleetwood Hotel on the North Quay, Douglas. The guests were roused and the alarm given. The small engine belonging to the Sun Fire Office arrived but it proved totally inadequate against the fire, which was by now threatening adjoining property.

Another machine, built privately by John McGhie, a Douglas brassfounder, also came and proved to be a powerful engine. It was manned by fishermen and marines from *HMS Torch*, moored in the harbour. After a lot of strenuous work the fire was put out.

Setting Sun

The Sun engine was much criticised, and people deplored the fact that the town did not have an efficient engine of its own. The era of the insurance brigades was clearly coming to an end.

A public meeting was called in Douglas Court House on October 12, 1848, by High Bailiff Quirk. The meeting resolved to purchase the Grampus engine, manufactured by Messrs McGhie, Teare and Lewthwaite, for £80, and to provide a further £50 for hose, buckets and branch pipes. A committee was elected under the chairmanship of the High Bailiff to administer the engine and raise the necessary money by public subscription. The committee included Mr Dumbell and Messrs Bluett and Harris, both of whom later became High Bailiffs of Douglas.

The Sun Fire Office was among the subscribers, donating £15 towards the cost of the new engine. On November 2, the insurance company sold its own engine for £5-19s-6d and donated the proceeds to the fund for maintaining the new engine, in the process ending the Sun Insurance Brigade in Douglas.

During the same month, the Grampus was purchased and placed in the Court House for the use of the town. The old engine was removed, having been found to be useless.

The last fire attended by the Sun Insurance Brigade was at the premises of Mr Qualtrough on the North Quay on November 1. Water was again a problem and the turnkey, or waterman, did not arrive until after the fire was put out. It was the waterman who held the key to the fire plugs positioned around the town. The press urged that the alarm should be given to the waterman at the same time as, or even before, the firemen.

The importance of this was realised later when duties were laid down for police constables in 1879: they had to know the position of all fire plugs. Constables who had the officers of the waterworks living on their beat were instructed to give the alarm to the engineers or persons in charge of the waterworks before doing anything else.

The first fire attended by the new Douglas town engine was at Duke Street, in December, when a strong wind made conditions difficult. Unfortunately, the engine was slow in getting started because it was the first time a new hose had been used. Once it was in operation, the fire was soon under control.

The small Sun fire engine, sold in 1848, did not leave the Island. It was bought by the Moore family, who had been the Douglas agents of the Sun Fire Office from the outset, and it was used by them at their Tromode sailcloth works.

Fire broke out on April 19, 1856, at premises in Hanover Street, Douglas, used by William Kelly, a soap-boiler and tallow chandler. It was discovered shortly after 2am and Chief Constable Sayle, together with other constables, brought the fire engine from the Court House. There was some delay in getting water from the town mains, but once the engine was working it was put to good effect. The fire, however, continued to burn fiercely, being fed by the tallow in the works.

Mr W F Moore, still the agent for the Sun Fire Office, heard of the fire and immediately sent his private engine from Tromode, coming down with his men to work it. Finding that nothing could be done to save the building, their efforts were directed at saving adjacent properties.

A large warehouse opposite was in great danger; plaster on the gable of the building cracked with the heat, paint blistered and windows shattered.

The fire was eventually extinguished at 6am. The premises were insured for £2,000 and the stock for £1,750 with the Sun Fire Office. It is interesting to note that the old Sun engine was still serviceable, although in private ownership, some eight years after it had been the centre of fierce criticism. Clearly this criticism had been directed at the larger of the two original engines, of which no further record exists.

Now it was the turn of the Grampus to give cause for concern. There was no-one appointed to look after it and the only time it was taken out of the engine house was when it was needed for a fire. It was only then that the problems of neglect became apparent.

The engine was in the care of the High Bailiff and, in his capacity as the town's administrator, he called a meeting of insurance agents and other interested people to inspect and repair it.

The meeting was held in September 1856; by October, the engine had been repaired by John McGhie, one of those who originally built it. A hundred yards of $2\frac{1}{2}$" flax hose in four lengths — complete with branches and couplings — were supplied by the Liverpool and London Insurance Company through its local agent, Mr H Johnson. The engine was thoroughly tested in front of the High Bailiff and found to be in first class condition.

Though the engine continued to be used, the equipment began to show signs of neglect and the people who turned out with the engine did not always understand how it worked. This state of affairs was deplored in contemporary reports, which advocated a corporate body to manage the affairs of the town. This came about four years later, in 1860.

Where Douglas leads...

Meanwhile, the other towns were in varying states of preparedness for fighting fire. Ramsey and Peel had no cover, while Castletown had the militia. Outbreaks of fire drew attention to this potentially perilous situation and highlighted the need for fire-fighting organisations which would be enabled by the various Town Acts.

The Sun Fire Office had spent money on repairs to its Ramsey engine in January 1827 and October 1831, but there are no references to the engine being there after 1850. Ramsey no longer had an engine, and the town made no efforts to provide one by public subscription.

In August 1856 there was a fire in Ramsey. It could have had very serious consequences and provoked criticism about the lack of a proper fire brigade. The fire broke out in the Lane &

Company brewery; flames were seen coming out of the upper windows shortly after 10.30pm, when the alarm was quickly raised.

Mr Bennett, head constable of Ramsey, was one of the first on the scene. He organised a bucket chain from a nearby public pump. Another bucket chain was set up from a well inside the brewery yard, but the flames, fanned by a strong breeze, soon gained the upper hand.

Adjoining property was soon threatened by wind-borne embers. A wooden downspout on an adjacent house caught fire; the house was pulled down to stop the fire spreading. The police organised patrols to protect property and extinguish small roof fires.

The fire had started when a timber floor ignited from contact with an overheated boiler flue. Brewery employees, realising the fire was still under the boiler, fought their way in and drew the boiler fire. The boiler was glowing red and, fearing an explosion, workmen braved the burning roof timbers to climb to the top and lift the safety valve. Their courage prevented a very serious explosion. The roof fell in at 2am, the fire eventually burning itself out two hours later.

Castletown still relied on military personnel for its cover, and they were in action at a fire in May 1857, attended by the Barracks' engine. Fires in Douglas in the same year showed up problems with the water supply. One fire occurred in Hill Street, at Radcliffe's cabinet-maker's workshop. The alarm was raised shortly before 10pm. Chief Constable Sayle was quickly on the spot and the fire engine was brought up from Lower Church Street. The fire proved too fierce for the engine to have any effect, due to low pressure in the water mains. The building was gutted and the large number of helpers who had brought the engine were unable to assist.

EARLY EQUIPMENT: Pictured right, top, are firemen's hand paraffin lamps manufactured by John Morris, of Manchester, and supplied to the Douglas brigade around 1900. The lower photograph shows the type of helmet worn by members of the brigade at this time. See also over.

The Douglas brigade with Raglan, its horse-drawn fire engine. The Merryweather Greenwich Gem had a pump driven by a double-cylinder vertical engine operating at 120psi, and was bought new in 1909 for £320.

2. The Town Acts

Local authorities are given fire-fighting powers

THE FIRST LEGISLATION giving power to a local authority to spend money on fire fighting apparatus was contained in the Douglas Town Act of 1860. In it the Commissioners were given the necessary means "to hire or purchase suitable premises wherein to keep fire engines, to purchase and support fire engines and all necessary appliances thereto, to appoint a fire brigade and determine their pay and charges...".

The Douglas Town (Amendment) Act of 1864 extended these powers to enable the insurance companies to be charged for the services of the town's brigade and appliances attending fires at insured premises. There were provisions for apportioning costs where more than one company was involved, and means of recovering costs in the event of disputes.

The Commissioners were also empowered to permit the fire engines to attend fires outside the town boundaries, and to charge for this service. For the first time, powers were given to constables and firemen to break into properties thought to be on fire, without the consent of the owner.

Castletown had been the centre of government and ancient capital of the Island, but in 1862 Douglas became the administrative capital. These towns, together with Ramsey and Peel, were still the four principal centres of population.

Town Acts followed, for Ramsey in 1865 and for Castletown and Peel in 1884. They all incorporated powers similar to those in the Douglas Act. Legislation was also introduced in the same period to permit the formation of water supply companies. It required these companies to provide fire plugs and to permit water to be taken free of charge at all times for fire-fighting. These water companies were later to provide hydrants of the "ball" variety.

Douglas Town Commissioners were the first to implement the provisions of their legislation. The first meeting of the newly elected Commissioners was held in August 1860 at the Court House in Athol Street, where it was agreed that a brigade should be set up. The fire engine, it was decided, could be stored under the Commissioners' new offices in St Barnabas Square, which were to be rented from Samuel Harris.

High Bailiff Bluett attended the meeting and informed the Commissioners that the fire engine which had been purchased by public subscription in 1848 was still in his charge; he felt he should hand it over to their care.

The High Bailiff also attended the next meeting and told the Commissioners that he wanted the engine moved from the Court House, where it had been kept since its purchase. The Commissioners were anxious to take it into their charge, but had nowhere to keep it. The engine was eventually housed in Callister's Yard at the west end of Athol Street, and initially placed under the care of the Town Clerk. The Commissioners decided to form a brigade of some 20 to 30 men and to purchase a length of hose and a stand-pipe.

The first properly constituted fire brigade for Douglas was formed in 1871. Before this date the brigade consisted of men employed by the Commissioners and any volunteers that could be mustered. The engine and equipment were maintained by the overseer under the direction of the Town Clerk.

On the evening of Tuesday, January 5, 1864, the chairman of the Council, John Mylrea, interrupted a meeting with a report of a fire in a stable at Derby Castle. Charles Craine, the Town Clerk, and John Robertson, the overseer, immediately rushed out into St Barnabas Square to accompany the engine to the fire.

The stable roof had fallen in by the time the fire brigade and the engine arrived, but contemporary reports tell us that the engine was used to throw water on the smouldering ruins. Captain Goldie and Inspector Sayle, together with other constables, controlled the crowd and helped to fight the fire.

Later in the month the Town Clerk was walking along the quay, as was the fashion, when he saw smoke pouring from the forepeak of the schooner *Jane and Agnes*, moored alongside. He quickly ran to the stores and brought the hose from the fire engine. With the help of passers-by, he connected it to the hydrant normally used for replenishing Steam Packet vessels. Members of the brigade were soon on the spot and broke through a bulkhead into the crew's quarters. After an hour they had extinguished the fire, which had been caused by a stove overheating.

So Douglas now had an efficient fire brigade under the charge of the Town Clerk. Tradesmen employed by the council made up most of the retained brigade, their knowledge of the construction of buildings proving invaluable when dealing with fires.

The lower part of Douglas, huddled round the harbour, was densely populated; many houses were built back-to-back, with a common yard serving two or three properties. Others were built around a courtyard. In such circumstances, fire could be very hazardous, and the priority of these early firemen was to stop fires spreading. An incident later that year illustrates the point.

Two brothers by the name of Kaye ran a dye and silk-processing works at the rear of a shop (owned by a Mr Johnson) in Duke Street. Fire was discovered at 10.30am on Monday, June 12. The alarm was raised and the fire brigade were soon at the scene. The men attached the hose to a plug in King Street, to the rear of the burning building. Helped by a good supply of water, the fire was prevented from spreading to nearby premises, and the flames were extinguished in half an hour. But the three-storey building was gutted and the mangles, presses, washing machines and rollers, used for pressing shawls, were all destroyed.

A horse stabled in the lower part of the building was rescued and two other horses owned by Mr Clague, the coal merchant, had to be moved from a stable in the lane opposite.

Fear on four legs

The presence of animals, with a natural fear of fire, was another hazard for the fire-fighters. Nine horses were less fortunate when fire struck at Ballamoar, Patrick. Sparks from a portable steam engine used in threshing were thought to have set light to straw. The resulting fire spread through the stackyard and engulfed the adjacent buildings. The horses suffocated before they could be rescued, but 20 cattle were saved.

Thomas Kinrade, of Ballafageen, Michael, was unluckier. He went to Ramsey on business; soon after he left, a fire started in a haystack and quickly spread through the stackyard. The smoke alerted neighbours who ran to the farm and tackled the fire. Despite their strenuous efforts, the corn in the stackyard, valued at £300, was destroyed.

Ramsey received its Town Act in 1865 but it was no help to Daniel Kelly and William Corlett who were in partnership as joiners, millers, agricultural engineers and general dealers in Kirk Michael. Late in May 1866 their premises were destroyed by a fire which started in the sawmill. It quickly spread to the tower of the windmill and the threshing mill. The machine shop, housing several partly-completed threshing machines and other agricultural implements, was soon engulfed. Fanned by a strong breeze, the fire spread to timber stored in the yard and to the rear of cottages in Windmill Terrace. With the mill lost, the villagers tried to save the houses.

In the meantime the fire bridged the land behind them and set fire to outbuildings at the rear of the Post Office, belonging to John Cameron. There was great confusion in getting cattle out of the buildings; the fire spread so quickly that one cow perished before it could be reached.

The spread of fire was eventually stopped by the continued efforts of the villagers. The mill was, however, completely burnt out.

An inquiry was held at Kirk Michael Court House, on June 14, under the direction of R J Moore, High Bailiff of Peel. After hearing all the evidence, he found that the fire had been the result of arson, and that the motive was revenge. A public meeting at

A 60-foot Curricle wheeled escape built by Shand Mason in 1895, and acquired by Ramsey Brigade for £69 7s. It is now on display at the small museum of horse-drawn equipment at Strathallan, Douglas.

the Mitre Hotel in July opened a fund for Kelly and Corlett. The sum of £40 was immediately subscribed, a clear indication of the value of the firm as employers in the area.

In December 1865, Mr Blackwell, printer and bookseller, of Malew Street, Castletown, was preparing for a family Christmas

with his family. He was getting out of bed when one of the servants roused the whole household, having discovered a fire in a child's bedroom. The alarm was raised and the fire engine and military personnel, commanded by Major E J Dickenson, were soon on the spot. By their efforts, and with the help of neighbours, the fire was confined to the upper storeys and extinguished — but not without considerable damage to the shop and contents below.

Meanwhile the militia were having more to do with the affairs of the Island than with fighting fires. Major Dickenson wrote to the High Bailiff of Castletown and informed him that he had issued a district order preventing his troops from helping to fight fires outside the Barracks, and advising that the fire engine would not be used for fighting fire in the town or its neighbourhood.

The High Bailiff immediately wrote to Governor Loch, informing him of the order, pleading that the only fire engine in the town was the one at the Barracks, and asking him to bring pressure on the military to continue to provide a fire-fighting service.

Early on the morning of Friday, July 27, 1866, a fire was discovered in Moore's bakery, which was part of the Douglas Hotel in Market Place. The alarm was immediately raised and messengers sent for the fire brigade; it soon arrived with the engine. When the shop door was forced open, the interior was found to be fiercely ablaze. The flames broke through the ceiling and into the hotel, so the brigade tried to contain the fire by tackling it from inside the hotel.

After much strenuous effort, the fire was extinguished. However, the shop interior was gutted and an oyster stall, kept in the basement by John Cowley, was severely damaged.

Although the Douglas Brigade continued to function efficiently, Governor Henry B Loch wrote in 1869 to Captain Goldie, the head constable, asking him to prepare a scheme for the formation of a full-time fire brigade for Douglas.

By December the Governor had authorised Captain Goldie to take charge of the fire engine and hose and to form a fire brigade for the town. The council was to pay an annual sum of £10 to the

Police, together with any payments received from insurance companies.

The Town Commissioners had agreed to these conditions and to contribute £20 annually towards the expenses. Yet nothing came of all this, as far as the police were concerned, and the Island — unlike many places in the British Isles — never did get a police brigade.

The Commissioners moved the engine and apparatus to their yard in Fort Street in November, 1869, and put everything in a good state of repair. They fixed a revised charge of £5 for the use of the engine and hose, whether used separately or together. The positions of all plugs and hydrants were marked on walls. However, the state of the brigade was not good and this problem was to occupy much of the committee's time during the next year. The outcome was the drawing-up of the first set of rules and regulations for the fire brigade.

On May 12, 1871, William Kewley, a mason by trade, was appointed the first captain of the Douglas Fire Brigade.

Over the next few years the brigade functioned well, attending a number of serious fires. Two of the most severe occurred in 1875. One gutted the entire coach-building establishment of Cringle & Fell, of Wellington Square. The brigade fought strenuously to contain the fire and stop it spreading to Curphey's grocery warehouse, next door. The other fire broke out in a paint workshop on Well Road Hill, belonging to Mr W Nicholson. The brigade arrived within 20 minutes but the flammable nature of the contents meant that little could be done to save the property.

Despite their ability, William Kewley was having difficulty keeping his men together. The reason was simple: they weren't getting paid! In fact, the men were owed a total of £56-9s -3d from various insurance companies for the services of the brigade. Matters came to a head in July when the Commissioners paid the men themselves and instituted proceedings for the recovery of the outstanding amounts.

Fires in some of the taller houses of Douglas were giving concern to the Commissioners. In January 1877 the Lighting and Cleansing Committee recommended to the full Board that a 50ft wheeled fire escape be purchased. David Munroe, now the head constable, sent the Commissioners a copy of Merryweather's illustrated catalogue for their consideration. In June they bought a 50ft Clayton fire escape and fly-ladder, a double stand-pipe and a felt helmet for the Superintendent of the brigade.

A fire at Pulrose Mill demonstrated that the Grampus manual engine was getting old. It was both heavy and unreliable, so a recommendation was made in September 1883 to buy a manual fire engine from William Rose & Company. The order, not placed until the following April, was for for a 14-man, 18cwt engine, complete with suction mechanism and modern patent coupling delivery hose. The cost was £95.

On July 14, William Kewley was told at about 11pm that there was a fire at Derby Castle. The brigade borrowed a horse and took the reel cart to the fire. On arrival they found no water supply. The cart had to be taken up Burnt Mill Hill to Strathallan Park Road where there was a hydrant. The brigade laid out 400 yards of hose over the cliff to the fire which was confined to gorse on the cliff face. It was 2am before the fire was out.

It is interesting to compare the names of the firemen who attended this blaze with the subsequent development of the brigade.

Superintendent: William Kewley

Firemen: Richard O'Hara, Mark Kelly, James Caugherty, William Moughtin, George Moughtin, Joseph Moughtin, Joseph Clarke, James Woods, Henry Sayle, Isaac Corlett, Daniel Clague.

The new engine arrived late in August 1884. It was successfully tested in Circular Road, throwing a jet of water over the Templar Hall, and was formally named *The Douglas*.

Its first active service should have been on August 26, when there was another fire at Derby Castle. The blaze was discovered at 10pm by the manager who sent a messenger on horseback. Kewley got his men together at the engine house and made the new engine ready. He sent one of the men for a pair of horses and, after trying several places, he reported back that none could be found. Eventually, the brigade used Joseph Moughtin's van with one horse and took its hose and stand-pipes to the fire. This time the fire was more difficult to tackle and property was at risk. The fire on the cliff was not extinguished until 7am. It was the fifth call of the summer and arson was suspected.

Early in 1885 came the first instance of the Douglas Brigade operating outside the town, as permitted under the Town Act, when there was a fire at Peel. (Although Peel had its Town Act, it still had no fire brigade; it was to be five months before it was formed.) At 6.30pm on Tuesday January 13, a paraffin oil lamp was upset in an upper room of the Marine Hotel, one of the oldest hotels in Peel. Mrs Froy, the licensee's wife, was rescued by some of the men who were drinking in the bar.

The chief constable of Peel, Mr Cringle, together with constables Quirk, Clucas and Callan, was quickly on the spot. Seeing the threat to surrounding property, and knowing there was no fire brigade or fire-fighting apparatus in Peel, Cringle immediately telegraphed for assistance from Douglas Fire Brigade. Meanwhile, several of the Peel Town Commissioners, Messrs Joughin, Mylchreest and Keig, organised men to contain the fire. Captain Quigley, of the Royal Naval Reserve, arrived with men from the Battery and gave assistance.

The Douglas Brigade, under William Kewley, set off with the new engine and a full complement of men. When they arrived at Peel they found the hotel gutted, but still burning fiercely and threatening adjoining property. By 11.30pm, the fire was under control; it was out shortly afterwards.

At the end of 1887 the Douglas Brigade bought a new reel-cart, against a background of concern on the part of the Commissioners as to the brigade's efficiency. The Commissioners' Lighting and Cleansing Committee reported to the Board that the brigade's manual engine was in perfect order, the fire escape ladders and buckets were being painted, and the old hand-cart and reel-cart were to be repaired at once.

Further approaches were made to the police to take over the fire brigade, but Col Paul rejected them, having sought advice from various counterparts in England. He also referred to the correspondence of 1881 and pointed out that, at that time, it was the Commissioners who could not agree to a take-over of the fire brigade. The Commissioners had another try with the newly appointed head constable, Col Freeth, in November 1888, but to no avail. The era of the police fire brigades was clearly over.

The Peel Brigade

The newly constituted Peel Commissioners held their first meeting on May 15, 1884, and immediately set about implementing the provisions of the Town Act. But it was the following January before any progress was made towards forming a fire brigade, with a quotation for a fully equipped engine being obtained from Wm Rose and Sons of Manchester.

The engine — comprising just a hand-cart, with two stand-pipes, two reels and 150 yards of hose — was bought in June. Mr Joughin was the chairman of the Fire Service Committee and he sought the advice of Captain Quigley, the man in charge of the Rocket Brigade, about forming a fire brigade. The new equipment was stored in the Rocket Brigade House and most of Captain Quigley's men duly formed the new brigade. William Kermode was appointed Captain, at an annual salary of £5, on December 1, 1885.

Castletown Commissioners met for the first time on May 13, 1884, and concerned themselves with improving the town's sanitation. As far as fire-fighting went, the town was somewhat spoilt, having enjoyed the protection provided by the military barracks. But a fire in the town the following year led to Major Fritz-Herbert at the barracks expressing concern that his men could not function properly as a fire brigade while they had to rely on their manual engine. He wrote to the Commissioners, asking for a stand-pipe to be provided for use on the plugs in the town. When this was discussed with the Castletown Water Works Company, it emerged that the plugs were not adapted to take a stand-pipe.

The incident which had given rise to the Major's concern was a fire in Malew Street, at which the military had considerable difficulty maintaining a supply of water to the engine.

The fire was discovered about 10.30pm by Mr Wood, who lived above his drapery shop. The fire spread so rapidly that he and his family only just managed to escape. The alarm was raised, the engine was brought from the barracks and the soldiers quickly brought water onto the fire.

Adjoining property was threatened and the shutters and

windows of houses on the opposite side of Malew Street were set alight. The soldiers, with the help of townspeople, continued to work the engine until 5am. Water was obtained from a fire plug in the street and supplemented by a bucket chain from a nearby well.

The premises were gutted and several houses damaged. It was the worst fire in Castletown since King William's College burnt down in 1844. A dinner was given the following Monday to thank the soldiers and those who had helped fight the fire. In October, John Gilbert, Chairman of the Commissioners, called for the provision of an efficient fire engine for the town. The insurance companies were invited to subscribe towards the cost,

but the matter was dropped when no financial help was forthcoming.

Although Ramsey had received its Town Act in 1865, it was 19 years before the Town Commissioners provided a fire brigade. In February 1884 they opened negotiations with the insurance agents in the town, asking them if they would contribute towards the cost of equipment. The response was poor, with only the Isle of Man Insurance Company offering to put £20 towards the cost of the appliances, which was estimated at £50. A minute dated February 3, 1885, states that it was resolved that the company would enjoy free use of the equipment, but there were no details of what this comprised.

3. Death by fire

The Local Government Act, 1886; double tragedy prompts new rules

THE PUBLIC Health Act of 1884 had incorporated many requirements for sanitation and health, and it was the responsibility of the Commissioners of the various districts of the Island to enforce them. It also repeated and amended some of the requirements of the various Town Acts. The authorities were kept busy removing pigs from houses, keeping infectious disease at bay and generally improving the living standards of the Islanders.

But the amount of legislation was becoming unwieldy, and an Act was introduced to consolidate the various statutory provisions. Whereas previous legislation had given Commissioners the power, should they wish, to borrow money to buy fire-fighting equipment, the Local Government Act of 1886 made it compulsory for them to do so.

The Act gave the firemaster the power of entry and to close streets. It was his duty to report back to the Commissioners who, in their turn, were given powers to recover costs.

After their various attempts to interest the police in providing an efficient fire brigade for the town, the Douglas Town Commissioners were now faced with a statutory obligation. In January 1889 a sub-committee presented a report on the reorganisation of the Douglas Brigade, advising that a fire station should be established with a superintendent permanently on call.

By 1890 Richard O'Hara had become captain of the fire brigade. He lived in Queen Street, and it was there in October that year that he was to face the most difficult fire since his appoint-

LEFT: The year is 1901 and the occasion is a parade to celebrate the coronation of King Edward VII. The horse-drawn manual pump, The Douglas, was built by Wm Rose & Co. Taken in John Street, Douglas, near the fire station.

ment. The fire broke out in a jam-preserving works in Thomas Cubbon's general grocery stores which fronted onto the North Quay and backed onto Queen Street. The fire had a firm hold when the brigade arrived shortly after 2am and it was another four hours before it was under control. It penetrated an adjoining grain warehouse and the firemen had to fight the blaze from within the building as well as from the front and rear.

The top three storeys of Mr Cubbon's building were completely gutted. Twenty five tons of jam were destroyed and hams, meat and other groceries damaged by water. The adjoining premises suffered fire and smoke damage.

In September 1894, Mr Fielding, the headmaster of Hanover Street School, raised the alarm when he noticed that Kneen Brothers' drapery shop was on fire early one Sunday morning.

Inside were James and Joseph Kneen, their assistants Godfrey Green and Fred Cannell, and their housekeeper Miss Corlett. Sgt James Bell blew his whistle to wake them, but the staircase was ablaze and they could not get down.

James Kneen found a rope and they all managed to escape, although Miss Corlett was so frightened that she had to be forced out of the window.

By the time Richard O'Hara arrived, flames were bursting out of the windows. A plate glass window in a shop across the street cracked with the heat, and the occupants of Cowin's bakery could not escape from above the shop as the flames reached across the side street to their only exit. Mr O'Hara rescued them from the second floor window using the fire escape.

Meanwhile the brigade was fighting the fire with a good supply of mains water. Mr O'Hara and Edward Corlett were directing water onto the fire from the wheeled escape when part of the side string of the ladder collapsed. They had to hold on to the remaining side until they could be rescued from this precarious position. The fire was under control by 5am; two hours later it was completely out.

The damaged fire escape was repaired and the newly-appointed Town Surveyor, Mr Taylor, indicated that protection from the weather was required for the fire appliances. He was instructed to make the necessary arrangements.

Following this fire, the Commissioners considered the provision of additional fire escapes for the town. In October 1894 they decided to buy a patent Kingston 46ft fire escape and hose-cart for £55 and one patent Curricle 29ft fire escape for £36, from William Rose & Sons of Manchester. The equipment arrived in January.

The other escape, now repaired, had a reach of 45ft and an additional 10ft by using its fly ladder. It was stored with the other equipment in the new engine house in Thomas Moore's Livery Stables on the corner of Westmoreland Road and Circular Road.

During 1895 there were a number of fires which vindicated the choice of Circular Road for the engine house. Mr O'Hara now lived in Circular Road and eight of his men lived within 100 yards of him. With a downhill run into town, the attendance times improved tremendously. There were still occasions, however, when the police had put the fire out before the brigade arrived.

In August, police helped the brigade put out a fire at a tobacco factory in Seneschal Lane. Later that month, Sgt Corkish was on his walk (later known as a beat) when he saw smoke coming from the top storey of Mrs Butterfield's lodging house in New Bond Street.

But his attempts to warn the landlady were met with abuse, as she slammed the door shut. By this time flames were coming from the upstairs windows; people living on the upper floors could not get down the staircase and were calling for help. The fire brigade came to their rescue with the reel-cart and the fire escape.

The fire had been started when an old woman knocked over a candle and set fire to her bed. Though overcome by fumes, she was eventually revived.

Death fire brings changes

A fire on September 13, 1895 had tragic and far-reaching consequences. Sgt Fayle and Constable Faragher were walking down Victoria Road early in the morning when they smelled burning. As they got to the corner of Broadway they heard screaming and saw that one of the boarding houses in Sherwood Terrace was on fire.

The policemen roused the house and were told that two servant girls were in the attic. The officers ran upstairs but were beaten back by flames.

Half an hour later, Supt O'Hara arrived with the reel-cart. The fire escape arrived shortly afterwards and was pitched against the building. Water was played on the fire, which had now spread to the adjoining building. With the fire subdued, the men could force their way into the attic bedrooms and put the fire out.

The servant girls died in the fire. The inquest heard that their only means of escape was a trap-door. It also found that the party wall between the adjoining buildings had been reduced to a timber lath and plaster partition in the roof space; this had allowed the fire to spread to the neighbouring property.

These two facts had important legal repercussions: regulations were introduced to govern habitable rooms and bye-laws were prepared to cover the design of new buildings.

The efficiency of the fire brigade was also questioned and George Taylor, Civil Engineer to the Town Commissioners, indicated at the inquest that a fire station was to be incorporated into the new municipal buildings, and so bring the brigade nearer the centre of the town.

The wheeled escapes were also relocated, after the fire, to different parts of the town. The tallest escape was placed at the Villiers Yard, convenient for the highest buildings on the promenade. The 45ft escape was put at the foot of Broadway and the smallest one was positioned in Kensington Road, to serve upper Douglas and the Bucks Road area.

Meanwhile, things began to happen in the village of Port Erin, a quiet place until the railway arrived in 1874. A breakwater was constructed, large hotels and boarding houses were built and suddenly services were needed. To organise this, the Port Erin Sanitary Authority was formed in 1884, later becoming the Village Commissioners who, in June 1896, decided to petition Tynwald for borrowing powers to purchase a fire escape and appliances.

They were doubtless inspired by memories of an incident 30 years earlier, when there had been a very serious fire in out-buildings at the Falcon's Nest Hotel.

A messenger was sent to Castletown to summon help, and soldiers under the command of Major Dickenson were dispatched with the Barracks engine. They arrived about 10pm, but it was 4am the following day before the fire was put out, due to the difficulty of getting water.

In March 1897 tenders were invited from Wm Rose & Company for the supply of suitable fire escapes. A 60ft Metropolitan escape was delivered in September at a cost of £91 4s. William Harrison, who was employed by the Commissioners, was put in charge of it and, by 1903, a brigade of 12 men had been formed.

Port Erin continued to expand and the Commissioners kept improving the public services, providing new sewers and water mains. By 1914 the reservoirs serving the district proved inadequate and the Commissioners petitioned Tynwald for borrowing powers to take over and expand the water undertaking.

This expansion had its effect on the fire brigade which had continued to function under Mr Harrison, relying mostly on his friends and fellow employees to assist as required. The escape had been kept in the Commissioners' yard and its condition was giving cause for concern. It was time for the brigade to be put on a proper footing.

A special meeting was held to discuss reorganisation and the purchase of additional equipment. After considering tenders from Shand Mason, H Simmis & Co and J H Newsham, the Commissioners agreed to buy a 45ft extending ladder and cart from Simmis at a cost of £72 9s. A letter was received five months later, in September, apologising for the non-delivery of the appliance due to pressure of work for the War Office. It eventually arrived on December 8, 1914.

The new brigade was to be made up of nine members, including the captain who was to be retained at a annual fee of £2 10s. In March, the Commissioners appointed William Harrison as Captain and the brigade members were G Costain, H Costain, J Costain, J Kelly, W Quilliam, A Cregeen and S Duke.

Port Erin now had an efficient brigade with a reasonable amount of equipment, including a wheeled escape and combined ladder cart and implement van.

All was not well in Peel, however, as the entire brigade had resigned in January 1887. The problem centred around pay and equipment and the captain was summoned to the next Commissioners' meeting for an explanation. His reasoning was accepted and he and the rest of the brigade were reinstated.

By 1890 the brigade was holding quarterly practices and functioning efficiently. The brigade members were William Kermode (Captain), R Callister, A Radcliffe, H Caine, T Kermode, J Kelly and T Quilliam.

The first record of attendance at a fire in Peel involved the premises of G B Kermode, cabinet-maker, in Market Street. The account for £7 17s was paid by the General, and the Manchester insurance companies. Over the next two years the brigade negotiated increased rates for attendance.

William Kermode resigned as Captain of the brigade in August 1895. Henry Quayle succeeded him, with Messrs Cowell, Wilson, Quirk, Jones and Thomas Watterson the members of the brigade. At the same time the Commissioners broke their ties with the Rocket brigade and moved the fire-extinguishing equipment to Philip Clucas's store in Station Road.

A fire in November 1896, at the Fenella Hotel at the foot of Peel Hill, illustrated the widespread problem of low water pressure as the towns began to develop faster than the water companies could improve their services.

In the case of the Fenella Hotel fire, the brigade had to run its cart three quarters of a mile from the blaze. But there followed another, more graphic, demonstration of the problem...

Peel was a small town; it was the centre of the Island's herring industry and houses rubbed shoulders with warehouses around the quay. In the larger warehouses were chandlers' stores and makers of nets and sails. Early in the morning of July 6, 1901, a warehouse belonging to William Teare, in Keown Lane, caught fire. It adjoined another warehouse belonging to John Keown, and backed on to yet another, owned by a Mr Higgins.

PC Cornish discovered the fire and called the brigade which was quickly on the scene and connected up to a hydrant. Access was difficult through back yards and lanes, and the water pressure was so poor that the firemen could not get near enough for the jets to reach the flames through the fierce heat. The warehouse was ablaze from top to bottom and the brigade could do nothing except concentrate all its efforts on stopping the fire spreading.

Henry Quayle was quick to enlist the help of bystanders to help move flammable material from the adjoining warehouses. They took buckets and extinguished the many small fires started by flying embers.

In his report, the Captain of the brigade expressed his frustration at being unable to fight a fierce fire effectively because of the low water pressure.

Thomas Watterson succeeded Mr Quayle as Captain in December the same year. He continued the fight to improve pressure in the mains; the brigade had no pumps and relied on mains pressure to throw water any distance.

In March 1902 Mr Watterson received a call to a fire at the station refreshment rooms. Within minutes the brigade was at the fire. There was some delay in finding a hydrant and there was poor pressure, but the men were able to get straight to the seat of the fire which was out within half an hour.

However, in his report to the Commissioners, Thomas Watterson complained again about the lack of pressure in the mains and the fact that hydrants had been covered by road metal.

The Commissioners' Committee of Improvements, Finance and Fire Brigade acted and by 1904 the water company had made some improvement. With the co-operation of the company's turn-key, the brigade now had the ability to throw water over the houses on Marine Parade.

Subsequent reports reflect how efficiency increased with the improvement in mains pressure. For example, a straw fire in cow sheds at the rear of the Vicarage was quickly extinguished; contrast this with problems outside the town when the brigade

had been called two years earlier to a fire at Knockaloe Mooar, Patrick.

The brigade ran some two miles to the farm with its hand cart. When the men got there they could not use their hose as there was no piped water supply and they had no pump.

Thomas Watterson reported: "We did all that was possible for us to do with our ladders and buckets until four in the morning." That was seven hours after the alarm had been raised. The building was gutted but the brigade had at least stopped the fire spreading to the farmhouse.

The brigade continued to operate out of its increasingly inadequate premises in Station Road — there was no facility for drying hose and it was difficult to get in and out with the ladder.

In 1912 the brigade was called to a fire in the Railway Hotel and, although it was quickly extinguished, some of the men were overcome by smoke. Thomas Watterson pressed the Commissioners to provide smoke helmets and two were subsequently bought from Eeds & Company, of Manchester.

Ramsey follows

Ramsey Commissioners were now under pressure to comply properly with the provisions of the Local Government Act. In June, the Commissioners bought, from Wm Rose & Co, a fire hand cart 25 yards of hose and two ladders. In October the Commissioners appointed Alfred Wall Brigade Captain at £4 a year.

A portable fire brigade engine with 30ft of suction hose and 12ft of delivery hose was ordered from William Clague's ironmongery warehouse on East Quay. Uniforms, ladders, 150ft of canvas hose and a jumping sheet were also obtained.

The brigade operated out of the old brewery until the completion of the proper station which was to be incorporated in a new Town Hall planned for Parliament Square.

Like their counterparts in Peel, Alfred Wall and his chief officer, William Boyd, were soon complaining bitterly about the lack of water pressure in many parts of Ramsey and the fact that some hydrants were set too deep for their standpipes — as well as requesting more hoses, helmets and boots.

Subsequently, the Commissioners bought a secondhand manual fire engine from Stourbridge Fire Brigade, Worcestershire. It was repainted and lettered at a cost of £10 and delivered in April 1888.

The brigade continued to function with the hand cart and manual engine, dealing with the small number of fires that Ramsey had come to regard as normal.

But in 1895 a spate of fires, most of them in the built-up area of Maughold Street, led to disputes with the insurance companies as to apportionment of costs. The Commissioners' Lighting and Cleaning Committee, which now administered the brigade, recommended that a fire escape should be bought in the interests of public safety. A Shand Mason Curricle Escape was ordered in November 1985 at a cost of £69 7s, but it was to be almost six months before it arrived at Ramsey on the *SS Ellan Vannin*.

The ladder, which could extend more than 60ft, comprised four sections, each of about 18ft. The lower two were braced externally and one slid within the other, whereas the top two were conventional. The whole assembly was carried on two large wheels and a hose cart with room for branches and standpipe.

The new escape was demonstrated to civic dignitaries and a large crowd of townsfolk at an unfinished property next to the Premier House on the North Promenade. Not only did it give access to a sixth floor window, but three firemen demonstrated the ladder's strength by climbing in close order. Another man climbed the ladder as it stood clear of the building, with two firemen holding the heel of the ladder.

In September the Ramsey Brigade was called to a fire outside the town which underlined the sort of problems of communication and access which faced both the public and the fire service.

George Morris, the tenant of the Slieau Lewaigue Hotel, found himself the victim of an exploding oil lamp which set fire to his bedroom. He and his family escaped, while a neighbour summoned the Ramsey brigade.

Neighbours gave what help they could, passing buckets of water upstairs to Mr Morris who was trying vainly to extinguish the fire. The burning oil was seeping through the floor into the public bar. Spirit bottles exploded, feeding the fire which now had a good hold on two floors at the west end of the building.

The brigade turned out with the escape and the engine; two horses were obtained from Mr J Lindsey, of Parliament Street. The hotel was at the top of a very steep hill and the road was rutted. So the brigade arrived with some difficulty shortly after midnight — one and a half hours after the fire had broken out.

The whole front of the building was found to be alight and part of the roof had fallen in. Captain Wall took the engine round the back of the building and positioned it alongside a small dub, or pond, fed by a stream. Two hoses were employed at once, but the water supply dried up just as the firemen were making some progress. The engine emptied the dub faster than the stream could fill it.

By 2am the building was completely gutted and the brigade could do little more than damp down with the limited water available.

The Lighting and Cleansing Committee took great pride in its brigade, but late in 1897 it was transferred to the newly constituted Stables and Stores Committee under the chairmanship of Mr W T Crennell.

The continuing problem of water pressure became so severe that Captain Wall and Superintendent Boyd decided to test a number of hydrants in the town during February 1900. Pressure at Lezayre Mount, Windsor Road and St Olave's was found to be good and a $3/4$" jet was sent over the steeple of the church. Pressure in the lower part of the town was not so good and, on the South Promenade, it was only sufficient to throw a $3/4$" jet a distance of 10ft. With a $1/2$" branch, water could barely reach the eaves of a two-storey house. The manual engine was connected up, but after half a minute it was starved of water. The matter was taken up with the Waterworks Company.

Captain Wall retired in 1900 and the brigade carried on under the leadership of its superintendent, William Boyd.

In June 1887, the question of providing suitable fire extinguishing appliances for Castletown was again considered and quotations obtained by the Commissioners, who nonetheless voted against purchase. Instead, they instructed their chairman,

Mr J Mylchreest, to discuss with officers at the Barracks to what extent the engine there could be relied upon for the town's use.

By August 1890 the Commissioners had still not complied with the statutory requirement to provide a fire engine for the town. A meeting with the water company was hastily convened and agreement reached for the conversion of the 17 existing fire plugs to ball hydrants and for an additional 20 such hydrants to be placed around the town.

At a special meeting of the Commissioners in August it was agreed to spend £50 on a hose and implement box, complete with tools and 450ft of hose, from Morris & Company, of Salford. Also included were one Regent hand-pump (Government pattern) and one set of Morris telescopic ladders to reach 30ft. Premises were rented in the Union Hotel Yard and Robert Clarke, the Town Clerk, was appointed firemaster.

The Commissioners meanwhile sent a deputation to Captain Gore at the Barracks to ask if the military authorities would reconsider giving their services and allowing the use of their engine at any fire which might occur in the town, pending formation of the brigade and completion of the hydrant conversion. The captain agreed, subject to their being allowed to connect the engine to the new hydrants and that the Commissioners pay for any damage to the soldiers' uniforms.

By April 1891 the town had been unable to raise a fire brigade despite having advertised for men. The Commissioners were obliged yet again to ask the military for assistance. Agreement was reached with Captain Ayde, the new commanding officer, that the military would provide a fire brigade for the town using the Commissioners' equipment or their own as required.

But in February 1896, the military authorities announced that personnel were being permanently removed from the town and that the Barracks were to close. Suddenly the Commissioners were faced with the problem of having to form their own fire brigade. A committee comprising Messrs Collister, Fell and Cannell was given the task.

Necessity proved the mother of invention and a brigade, under the captaincy of John Cubbon, was ready to take over from the military on February 14, the day after the troops' departure.

The manual engine in the Barracks dated from 1845; it had been left behind when the detachment of the North Lancashire Regiment left aboard the SS *Snaefell*. The Commissioners wrote to Col Hope, General Commanding Officer of the Western District, at Chester, offering £10 for the engine, which had been made by J Stone & Company of Deptford. The offer was accepted in June and the brigade had its first practice with the engine in July.

In December the following year, a farmworker discovered a fire in the threshing mill and the adjoining barn at Ballaglonney Farm, Malew. A lad was sent three quarters of a mile along the railway track to the station at Santon, where the station master telegraphed Castletown.

It took the brigade an hour and a quarter to cover the five miles to Ballaglonney, with the engine often sinking in the mud and deep ruts on the climb out of Ballasalla. By the time it arrived, the mill and barn were gutted, but the brigade was at least able to stop burning embers, blown by the wind, from igniting other buildings.

Towards the end of 1898 the fire station was moved to premises in Hope Street and responsibility for the brigade was transferred to the newly formed Stores Committee. Various pieces of equipment were purchased between then and 1911 when the brigade was re-organised. The most important were a standpipe and new hose fitted with patent instantaneous couplings bought in 1910 from John Morris & Sons. About the same time, the Commissioners opened negotiations to buy the old barracks and drill ground, and took possession in January 1912.

Tourist pressures

Douglas was expanding rapidly as a Victorian watering place, and as the end of the 19th century approached the number of seasonal visitors was nearing half a million. Most of the town's large houses were used as lodgings and many streets were given over entirely to boarding houses. The Loch Promenade was complete and the largest hotel on it was the Villiers.

All these buildings, and the many large places of public entertainment, presented a formidable task for the Superintendent of the fire brigade, Richard O'Hara, and his men, with their manual engine, ladder cart and street escapes.

The brigade was severely tested by a large fire in May 1898. Three young men walking along Duke Street in the early hours spotted flames on the ground floor of No 55 and sounded the alarm at Villiers Corner.

The brigade arrived at 2.30am to find that the fire had taken a fierce hold. The young men who had raised the alarm had, with great presence of mind, run the wheeled escape up from the Villiers Corner and had it ready for the brigade.

John Harvey and his niece were sleeping on the fourth floor of their house. Once awakened by a policeman's whistle, they tried to make their way down the staircase, only to be beaten back by flames and smoke.

Next door, Walter Halsall had been wakened by the commotion and was quick to see his neighbours' plight. He opened a third floor window, shouted to Mr Harvey and helped the pair out of the landing window onto the outlet roof and into his house.

He acted none too soon, for the flames quickly engulfed the building and the rescue, despite the best efforts of the young men, would have been too late.

The brigade soon had two hoses in use at the front of the building. There was no access to the rear of the property from Duke Street Lane, so a third hose had to be brought through Mr Halsall's property and the fire fought from a small yard at the rear.

The heat of the fire was intense and soon the roof collapsed. Adjoining property was severely damaged and the brigade was hard pressed to contain the fire. By 4am, however, it was under control and extinguished shortly afterwards.

The tar works tragedy

Shortly after 5pm on December 28, 1899, two apprentices were installing a new engine in the tar yard at Douglas Gas Works. One of the men borrowed a small moulder's lamp to soften some lead piping. As he walked past the ammonia tank, the naked flame ignited the vapour escaping from the vents.

The tank exploded, lifting the 4ft-thick concrete top high into the air. This was followed quickly by a second explosion in the washers and a third in the pipes between the purifiers and the retort.

The gas flared up in a tremendous fireball and the adjoining tall building housing the scrubber — a cast iron cylinder surrounded with brick — exploded. Portions of this building flew across the harbour and landed in Quiggin's yard almost three quarters of a mile away. A jet of gas from the damaged scrubber was burning freely, the flame rising to more than 100ft. A deafening roar could be heard all over the town.

Gas works employees, working in great danger, had to close valves leading from the gas holders. The retorts were drawn and the escaping gas from the mains extinguished as, one by one, the valves were closed.

As soon as the works were rendered safe, the fire brigade went in. The men extinguished the burning buildings and assisted with recovering the bodies of three men who had been killed.

A fire on Douglas Head in September 1900 highlighted some shortcomings of the brigade's equipment. The ability of the men, however, was not in doubt...

The Warwick Tower Pavilion was an iron bird cage-like structure 200ft high, with rotating observation lifts in which people rode. At its base was a boiler house and pay desk. There was a dance pavilion, amusement arcade and side shows, all built in timber. The engine house for the revolving lifts was also in a timber match-boarded building.

The brigade arrived with the manual engine less than half an hour after the alarm. The building was a mass of flames, with oil and grease in the boilerhouse adding to the fire.

Water was, as ever, the real problem — the town main finished some distance lower down the road opposite the Fort Anne Hotel. Captain O'Hara first used the roof storage tanks of the Douglas Head Hotel as his water supply, while the manual engine was connected to the end plug of the main.

The brigade commandeered extra help but, with the hand pump working under full pressure, it could not lift the water sufficiently to throw a jet on the fire.

Captain O'Hara found a well serving the Fort Anne Hotel and got permission to draw from it. He was able to lift water half a mile to the fire.

By this time the buildings were engulfed in flames reaching half way up the tower. The lift counterweights, each weighing five tons, came crashing down from the top of the tower. The impact sent sparks and burning embers flying over the Douglas Head Hotel.

The brigade concentrated its efforts on protecting the hotel, but the pavilion was gutted and the tower and lifts severely damaged.

Meanwhile, the new Town Hall had been built and opened at the beginning of May. The buildings included a fire station which housed the manual engine and a ladder cart. The Clayton escape was kept at the Villiers Yard and the other two escapes remained at Broadway and Kensington Road.

Fire underground

At the end of 1900 the Island had another major industrial fire, though this time without loss of life.

Foxdale was a remote mining village in the parish of Patrick, six miles from Peel and 11 from Douglas. It was the centre of the Island's mining industry; 12 mines worked the productive lead veins which also yielded a high silver content.

Christmas Day was the miners' only holiday. The mine buildings were quiet and only the watchmen were about. Shortly after daybreak, smoke was seen pouring from the top of Beckwith's shaft at the Old Flappy mine.

The watchman raised the alarm and woke the mine captain; word soon spread around the village. Men rushed to the mine and assembled at the head of the shaft, concerned as much for their livelihood as for the investment of the owners.

Remote from the towns and accustomed to fending for themselves, the miners formed teams and set about finding the seat of the fire. The first men to enter the mine were driven back at the 35-fathom level by the dense smoke.

The three principal shafts at Foxdale all connected at various levels. Captains Kitto, Lean and Collister took men down Bawdens and Potts shafts, securing each level as they went, until they reached the 170-fathom level. Here the fire was discovered, in a sump head in a cross cut. Water was a problem as well as the heat, and only one man at a time could get in to fight the fire.

Water was let down from a higher level and, by scooping it up in buckets and throwing it on the fire, the miners managed to contain the blaze in the one level, although it continued to burn for three days. Miners fought the fire in relays and many were overcome by smoke. They had to be carried 1,000ft up ladders by their colleagues to reach the surface.

On the third day the fire burnt through timber roof supports; the resulting rock fall smothered the flames. The fire had been caused by two men leaving their candles burning in their rush to get away on Christmas Eve.

In September 1902, a large fire at the Palace Pavilion in Douglas highlighted another problem for the Douglas brigade to add to its difficulties with water pressure.

The alarm was raised at about 2am and very soon the whole of the north gable of the huge ballroom was on fire. The seat of the fire was in the refreshment bar and it was thought to have started in a mineral water works at the rear of the Pavilion.

Soon the roof was alight and fire broke out at both ends of the building. Water was eventually obtained from a hydrant near Empire Terrace, but the brigade was handicapped because its ladders could not reach the roof, 85ft above floor level. Eventually, a long ladder normally used for servicing the arc lamps was obtained and the men were able to make some impression on the blaze. By 8am the fire was out.

In 1903 the brigade was again reorganised and a new set of rules was drawn up by the Town Clerk, Alexander Robertson, and the Borough Surveyor, A E Prescott.

The brigade was styled "The Douglas Corporation Fire Brigade" and was placed under the control of the Highways, Sewering and Works Committee and the Borough Surveyor. Richard O'Hara was appointed Superintendent and Station Keeper and paid 30/- per week; William Pickett was made

Captain on a retaining fee of £5 per annum.

Blaze at Laxey

In February 1905 there was a fire at the Queen's Hotel, Laxey, which provoked calls for the establishment of fire cover at this important village, mid-way between Douglas and Ramsey.

William Kinrade, whose mother was the licensee, raised the alarm in the village and the Douglas fire brigade was called by telephone. Mr Kinrade and friends tried to salvage what they could, but the fire spread quickly and soon they could not get near the bar or any of the upstairs rooms.

The brigade received the call shortly before 1am. Supt O'Hara obtained horses and left with the *Douglas* for the fire. They arrived at Laxey at 2.30am — once again their first problem was lack of water. The engine had to be moved further down Rencell Hill to the river, where 12 Laxey men took the handles to help raise water to the fire.

Their efforts were in vain — the fire had been too well established before the brigade arrived and they could do nothing to save the building. The local press carried leaders criticising the fact that Laxey had neither fire-fighting equipment nor mains water.

Things were a little better in Port St Mary, a village in the south of the Island which had grown around a busy harbour with a healthy fishing and boat-building industry.

Commissioners had been elected for the village district; they held their first meeting in April 1890. By 1900 the Rushen Water Works had some mains in the village and there were a number of hydrants. Two Commissioners were deputed to look into the question of fire fighting and, in December, a hose and standpipe were bought. The Commissioners considered forming a fire brigade in 1910 and asked the local police to supervise it, but nothing more came of the idea.

In Douglas, however, the fire brigade was being developed. Following strong representation from the fire brigade superintendent, the street alarms were removed in 1908. Complaints were being heard yet again about the poor water pressure in certain parts of the town, making it impossible for the brigade to function effectively.

The Borough Surveyor understood Richard O'Hara's predicament and asked the Highway Committee to provide a new fire engine, additional hose and two Pompier ladders.

The result was the purchase, in 1909, of a double-cylinder vertical Greenwich Gem fire engine from Merryweather and Company at a cost of £320. The new steam engine was ready to be inspected by the full Douglas Council on Thursday, March 4. The inspection took the form of a full scale drill at the Villiers Hotel.

Already the brigade had come up against snags: the engine was large and heavy and some of the town's streets were very narrow. It was designed to be hauled by three horses hitched abreast, but this presented difficulties when taking tight corners.

But at 3pm the new Merryweather Steam Engine was rolled out of John Street Station. Two horses from Gribbins' stables, normally employed on the Peel Road bus service, were yoked to swingle trees and pole. A lead horse was hitched to the pole in front of the other two, the fire was lit and the engine raced to the scene.

Supt O'Hara was in charge of the brigade, but the machinery was under the direction of a representative from the manufacturers.

A fine sweep was made into Prospect Hill and the superintendent blew his whistle to clear the way. The hill was climbed at a hard gallop and the engine turned into Finch Road. It gathered speed going down the hill and, on turning into Church Road, had to swerve to avoid a slow-moving coal cart. The back end of the engine skidded sideways into the pavement, lurching over and throwing two firemen and the Merryweather engineer off against the steps and into the railings of the houses in Church Road.

The engine was brought to a halt and Richard O'Hara ran back to check on his men. One had a sprained wrist; the other had injured his hip and could scarcely walk. Merryweather's man had a nasty gash in his right arm, but the jolt had also thrown the fire out of the boiler. They got back on the engine and were quickly underway again, running at full gallop down the centre of the Promenade. As they pulled across to the Villiers, a timber cart failed to give way and the driver had to swerve again, bringing the engine to a stop with the lead horse on its haunches and in danger of being run over by the pole horses.

Despite the eventful journey, the rest of the exercise went perfectly. The horses were unhitched, the fire was re-lit and two hoses connected to a hydrant and led into a canvas reservoir into which the engine suction was put. In four minutes the boiler pressure had reached 20lbs per square inch and after seven minutes a full pressure of 120lbs was reached.

The demonstration proved that the new engine could deliver more water than the mains could supply.

The brigade was able to become proficient in the use of its new engine before it saw use at a serious fire. This occurred at the site of its near disastrous skid on the first demonstration run.

The curate of St Thomas's Church was conducting the evening service on February 11, 1912, when he and members of the congregation smelled smoke. They thought no more about it, as fumes often came from the central heating boiler under the main part of the church.

The organist, Mr Poulter, played the recessional hymn at 7.40pm and he too noticed a strong smell of burning wood. He assumed it was coming from outside.

The Rev Robinson bade goodnight to his congregation and closed the main doors. Mrs Poulter joined her husband and was chatting to the sidesmen when they noticed that the burning smell was getting stronger. One of the men opened the door leading to the belfry; to his surprise and horror the whole of the belfry appeared to be on fire.

Mr Poulter and Mr Myerscough ran to the police station to raise the alarm. Some of the congregation talking outside the church looked up to see flames flickering through the louvres in the belfry, high in the tower above Church Street.

Suddenly there was a tremendous crash as one of the bells plunged through the floor of the belfry. Burning debris blocked the staircase, down which people had made their way just minutes earlier

The fire must have been smouldering on the floor above them during the service; it was the inrush of air when the main doors were opened that caused the belfry to burst into flames. They had all had a lucky escape.

It was 15 minutes before the fire brigade arrived. The first appliance to appear was the hand-cart, accompanied by six firemen. They connected a hose to a hydrant in Castle Street some distance from the church.

The crowd which had gathered heckled the firemen, shouting at them to use a hydrant in Church Street which was right outside the church. But the firemen were right. They had seen the flames leaping out of the tower as they ran along Strand Street and knew that they would need a lot of water. They also knew that there was an eight-inch main in Castle Street and that the one in Church Street was only a three-inch main.

Within a few minutes a jet of water was being played up the tower, but the strong easterly wind fanned the water into spray before it could reach the belfry. Another hose was run into the church and a ladder taken from the ladder cart, which was the next appliance to arrive, so that access could be gained to the gallery.

From the gallery the firemen were able to direct water into the heart of the fire, in the ringing chamber below the belfry, but with little effect. They also played water on the back of the organ to stop the fire spreading into the church. Within half an hour another of the great bells came crashing down and wedged itself in the head of the stairway. It was glowing red hot.

The men who had brought the ladder cart ran to Broadway and brought the wheeled escape; it was pitched on the north side of the tower from Church Road. The escape was not long enough to reach the belfry and fireman Crosby was standing on it when a roof-slate fell onto the escape below him. Supt O'Hara decided it was unsafe to use the escape and it was withdrawn. He put two men on the roof of the old vicarage; from here they could aim a jet into the louvres of the belfry.

Meanwhile concern was growing at the hospital, a quarter of a mile away at the top of Crellins Hill. When the first bell crashed down it sent showers of sparks high in the air which were blown over the hospital. A hose was made ready and hospital staff,

Mr I E Watterson, Captain of the Peel Brigade, with the horse-drawn manual fire engine, built by Shand Mason & Co, and bought secondhand by the Town Commissioners in 1921. Twenty two men were needed to operate it.

under the direction of Dr Lionel Wood, extinguished embers as they landed.

Shortly after 8.30pm the steam fire engine arrived, drawn by two horses. The boiler was lit to provide a head of steam. Hoses were connected but the wind was still turning the jets to a fine spray. The escape was brought back and pitched against the east side of the tower; from this position water from the steamer was poured on the fire, which was under control by 9.30pm.

One of the bells had fallen on the organ loft and efforts were made to stop the fire spreading into the main body of the church. The red hot bell was igniting the tinder-dry timber of the organ faster than the firemen could cool it. The heat from the bell melted the lead gutter between the tower and the chancel roof, which led to another minor outbreak of fire about 10pm. The firemen, who were now able to get closer to the fire, stopped it spreading to the main roof but in the process caused further damage to the organ.

The fire was the most difficult that the brigade had tackled; it was also the most spectacular. The sound of the bells crashing from the belfry, and the sparks shooting high in the air, soon attracted a large crowd.

The Douglas brigade had a full turn-out at this fire and all its equipment was in use. Three of the appliances belonging to the town were at the fire: a hand-cart (also known as the reel cart, which carried hose, some tools, standpipes and a small 18ft folding ladder); a ladder cart with two Pompier ladders and three scaling ladders; and the Merryweather steam fire engine. Also present was one of three wheeled escape ladders which were positioned around the town.

In August the following year the Douglas men again found themselves at Laxey, to fight a fire at the Glen Gardens pavilion. Within minutes of the brigade's assembly, the Captain, W J Pickett, procured a motor car. He took five men, some lengths of hose, a standpipe and some hand tools and left for Laxey. They arrived shortly after 1am, half an hour after receiving the alarm.

The speed of turn-out was commendable, but they were unable to do any useful work due to low pressure from the hydrants. The whole building, more than 100ft long and built of pitch pine, was one mass of flames.

Capt Pickett realised there was little that could be done until the steam fire engine arrived, so he left his men to contain any spread of fire while he surveyed the area to find the best location for the engine.

On arrival an hour later, it was taken through Corlett's Flour Mills into the gardens and placed beside an ornamental lake. With a good supply of water the fire was quickly brought under control. The pavilion, however, was totally destroyed.

Another fire, in April 1914 at Government House, is of interest. It was discovered about 11pm by Lady Raglan, who noticed a smell of burning coming from the servants' quarters. She and Lord Raglan immediately roused the household.

The fire was beneath the servants' quarters and the smoke caused some panic. A footman was overcome by smoke and had to be carried out by a manservant; a housemaid escaped through a window and down a ladder.

The Government Property Trustees had installed hydrants and hose eight months previously. Lord Raglan soon had his staff organised and the alarm was raised.

The Douglas Fire Brigade received the call at 11.15pm and Capt Pickett left by car with ten men. On arrival they found the Governor's staff were holding the fire in check. However, it broke through into the roof and proved difficult to control; a gas explosion injured firemen Quirk and Faragher. The fire was extinguished by 3am next day, but damage was considerable.

With the advent of the motor bus, the days of the horse bus were numbered. Douglas brigade now found it difficult to find horses for its steam fire engine. The council deliberated at length on the matter and, having lost a number of tram horses for war purposes, eventually resolved to supply horses from its depot in Lake Yard whenever required.

The annual report for that year tells us that there were 24 calls, two of them outside the town. In an effort to improve the brigade's efficiency, the council had authorised a night attendance at the fire station during the holiday season which increased the cost of the brigade to £350 for the year.

This is interesting when viewed in the context of a meeting which had been held at Government Office on April 20, 1912, attended by the Government Secretary, Mr B E Sargeant, and representatives of all the local authorities.

The purpose of the meeting had been to discuss a proposal to establish a professional fire brigade with two modern high-speed motor engines, stationed centrally to serve the whole Island. The villages and towns would retain only "first aid" appliances. The fire brigade would be under the control of the Chief Constable and the whole scheme would be funded by an Island-wide penny rate.

This would have produced an income of £1,650, which was considered sufficient to meet the expenses of a full-time brigade made up of a chief officer, second officer, two mechanics and eight firemen. The idea was clearly judged ahead of its time and rejected by the proud towns.

4. Defence of the Realm

The Local Government Consolidation Act, 1916

THE FIRE at Government House in the spring of 1914 had obliged the Governor and his family to move out until the damaged wing was rebuilt. They were accommodated by the Government Secretary, in whose residence they were living when war was declared in August.

The Defence of the Realm Regulations of the Imperial Government were adopted in the Isle of Man and the War Office immediately requested the Island to house alien prisoners.

Cunningham's Holiday Camp in Douglas was requisitioned and converted into an internment camp for "enemy agents". By October 1914 a total of 26,000 men, mostly merchant seamen, were kept there, four to a tent.

Emergency plans were drawn up involving the police, local authorities and fire brigades and, during October 1914, a Bill to consolidate all previous town and local government legislation was introduced in the House of Keys.

The Local Government Consolidation Bill eventually became law on July 5, 1917, after two years of the disruption inevitable for those living on a small island on the periphery of a World War.

The rise of Knockaloe

The Douglas camp was not the only, or indeed the largest, centre for internees. In 1914 the estate of Knockaloe, in the parish of Patrick, was requisitioned as an internment camp. Eventually it comprised 23 compounds, housing 1,000 men in each. By the end of 1915 its population was 26,000, including guards, engineers and civilian staff. A branch railway line was built to service the camp and to convey the internees who were brought to Peel by ship. The nearest fire brigade was at Peel and its equipment was one small handcart, a few buckets and ladder. The town lost a leading public figure on Sunday, January 23, 1916 when Richard O'Hara, the Superintendent of the fire brigade, died.

Soon after his death, the alarm bell system for calling the brigade was transferred to the fire station and. By June the system was centralised, with extensions in the Town Hall and the caretaker's flat.

On September 26, 1916 the Island received its first air raid warning against an impending Zeppelin attack. The fire brigades went to their allotted posts, but the alert passed without incident.

Notwithstanding the huge new population on its doorstep, the Peel brigade continued in much the same way as before. In March 1916 it was called to a fire not far from the camp at Knockaloe Farm. The men ran with the handcart almost two miles to the farm, and managed to contain a haystack fire.

Knockaloe was outside the town district and the Commissioners had no scale of charges for this type of service. They met, fixed a special scale, and sent an account for £6 11s 6d to the Commercial Union Assurance Company through its agent, Mr E T Christian. The company refused to pay and a legal argument began.

Meanwhile, the brigade had bought additional lengths of hose, fitted with $2^1/_2$" Morris couplings, from Keddaway & Company. Members were also issued with armbands.

At the end of the war the internees left the Island. The camp at Knockaloe was dismantled and the materials put to new uses. Some of the hut sections were still in storage at Walter Quayle's sawmill in Mill Road, Peel, in September 1920 when the brigade was summoned to a fire in the yard early one morning.

The huts, bought from the government by Roberts and

Armstrong, of Belfast, were well ablaze. The intense heat made it the worst fire the Peel men had tackled. Their limited resources were severely tested, as the fire spread to adjoining property; concern was even expressed for the safety of the gas works. Members of the brigade were sent to extinguish burning embers falling near the gas holders. The fire was eventually brought under control but, as dawn broke, the extent of the damage was seen to be considerable.

Later the same year the brigade found itself called to another farm fire outside the town boundary, this time at Shenvalley farm, Patrick. A total of 22 men fought the fire in a two-storey cow shed, putting it out after two and a half hours despite the lack of a good water supply.

In his report, Thomas Watterson requested the Commissioners to provide a manual pump if they wanted the men to keep attending fires outside the town boundary, where water could only be got from wells or streams.

The Commissioners did not act on the report and seemed unaware that their brigade had been tested to the limit on a number of occasions. The Local Government Board, however, was more aware of the situation. On January 21, 1921, it held a public inquiry which resulted in a reprimand for the Peel Commissioners for not enforcing their theatre regulations properly.

They were also told to provide a fire engine, as required under clause 271 of the Consolidation Act, and given three months to comply. The Commissioners lost no time in obtaining quotations for their new engine and eventually bought a secondhand London Fire Brigade machine, fully reconditioned, for £135.

The engine was a manual pump with two 6" gun-metal barrels fixed in a hardwood cistern with side lockers, hose and suction, designed to be operated by 22 men. It was intended to be hauled by a sway bar and pole with two horses. However, shortly after its delivery in June 1921, the brigade acquired drag ropes to allow it to be pulled by 20 men, it being found quicker to manhandle the engine within the narrow streets of the town.

On the first practice the engine threw a jet of water to a height of 120ft and was found to be entirely satisfactory. It was kept in the Commissioners' new yard at Boilley Spittal. The hose and ladder cart were also retained. The brigade captain's retainer was increased to £10 per annum and the brigade strength went up to 12.

Southern change

The Commissioners at Castletown had drawn up a set of theatre regulations in 1912 . They set about enforcing their provisions, having acquired the redundant barracks, as already described, and moved in their two appliances.

On the introduction of the new legislation, the Commissioners reviewed their equipment and satisfied themselves that they had adequate fire-fighting appliances. They considered the addition of a ladder but deferred its purchase.

A further review of the brigade was made in 1920 following a conference in Douglas which looked at the whole question of fire-fighting throughout the Island. The conference prompted the Commissioners to decide that their brigade should comprise younger men; they were concerned that interest in the brigade among its men was waning. So, on March 23, 1921 the old brigade was disbanded and a new one appointed, with James Kneale as captain.

Following his death, in May 1928, Thomas Corkill was appointed Captain. His several requests to the committee resulted in the purchase of an additional 100 yards of hose, chemical extinguishers for oil fires and a 40ft Ajax extension ladder. In the closed position the ladder was 24ft long and the fire station had to be altered to accommodate it. In 1932 the position of sub-captain to the brigade was created, and W Oates appointed.

There were few further changes in Castletown until 1939 when the Local Government Board advised the Commissioners that it intended to allocate funds to the town — under the Local Government Fires Bill, before Tynwald — for a Fordson Fire Brigade tender and trailer pump.

Meanwhile, the Local Government Board had also become aware of declining standards at Port Erin and reminded the Commissioners in 1927 of their statutory duty.

The Commissioners quickly recommended the appointment

of a new eight-strong brigade with a captain on an annual retaining fee of £8. They appointed Police Constable A Corris as Captain, subject to his Chief Constable's and the Government Secretary's approval. PC Corris took charge of the brigade in July but was deprived of his retainer on account of his police position.

After two practices, the captain requested the purchase of four extra lengths of hose and miscellaneous hand equipment including two Pompier ladder belts. He also reported that a number of hydrants had been covered over and should be exposed and marked by hydrant plates. The Commissioners agreed to both requests.

In 1934 the brigade moved into new premises which backed onto the police station. They had been converted from the redundant laundry of the Falcon's Nest Hotel.

The brigade saw action at two more major fires in 1936, at the Bay Hotel and the Imperial. The new captain, PC Lace, complained that mains pressure on the lower promenade was poor; at the Bay Hotel fire the hoses could not even reach the windows on the second floor.

The Commissioners had been considering improvements to the brigade appliances and these fires prompted the immediate installation of alarm bells. They also discussed the acquisition of a new motor tender.

At the same time, Port St Mary Commissioners suggested the two authorities should form a joint brigade, but Port Erin deemed the approach premature. PC Lace was transferred to St John's in due course. Following a well-established pattern, PC Arthur Cowin was appointed captain of the brigade in 1937.

Renewed approaches by the Port St Mary Commissioners coincided with moves by the Local Government Board to introduce new legislation. A number of meetings were held and the Rushen Fire Protection Order, 1938, made by the Local Government Board, saw the amalgamation of the two village districts and parish of Rushen for the purposes of fire protection.

The Rushen Joint Fire Protection Board was established under the chairmanship of Mr J Keggin, by an order approved by Tynwald in January 1939. It was financed by a rate levy of $1^1/_2$d in the £1.

The brigade at Port Erin continued under PC Cowin, but with only the old wheeled escape and hand-cart. Port St Mary still had the canvas fire hose in the box at the police station, and a hand-cart which had been bought in 1922 along with standpipes and hose.

Port St Mary appears to have shared Port Erin's difficulties in raising a fire brigade, and was the last important community on the Island to do so. In 1935 the Commissioners' fire committee, comprising Messrs Maddrell, Quayle and Kneen and James Cubbon, the Superintendent, was finding it difficult to hold practices.

By November 1936, however, James Crebbin had become Superintendent of a six-strong brigade, comprising also W L Kinley, W Kneen, James Hislop, C Faragher and James Oliver.

The last time the Port St Mary brigade attended a fire was Easter 1937 at a property in High Street, owned by a Mr Roberts of Glendown. It was obvious that new equipment was needed for the area.

It was not surprising that the new Joint Board made application to Tynwald in March 1939 to borrow £700 for a new motor appliance in the south of the Island.

The Palace blaze

The new legislation had not affected Douglas: the town had an efficient brigade and operated a reel-cart, ladder-cart, manual engine, several wheeled escapes and the steam engine.

Yet on July 13, 1920 the brigade was tested to its limit by a major fire at the Palace Ballroom. The ballroom had been rebuilt after a fire in 1902 and was now one of the finest in Europe. It had a beautiful parquet floor, and a large stage with dressing rooms and orchestra accommodation. It was connected by a corridor and vestibules to the Palace Coliseum and Opera House.

The alarm was first raised when a seal-keeper at the Coliseum was woken by the barking of his animals at about 3am.

The fire had started in the band-room at the rear of the ballroom and had a firm grip before the alarm was given. When the brigade arrived, shortly before 4am, the whole of the building was on fire and flames were breaking through the roof. It was clear the ballroom could not be saved and the brigade concentrated on stopping the fire spreading. The men demolished the connecting corridors between the ballroom and the Coliseum and brought hoses through to contain the fire. The roof collapsed and sent flames and burning embers 150ft in the air, threatening property in Palace Road.

By 6am the fire was under control, but the Palace was completely gutted. The brigade stayed in attendance all day, putting out the smouldering remains.

The Island felt the loss of this splendid tourist amenity very deeply. Although the Douglas brigade was praised for its efforts, the men felt frustrated that it had taken an hour from the receipt of the first call to get to the scene of the fire — a distance of just one and a half miles.

The station was manned at night during the summer season and W Pickett was employed full-time as brigade captain. His responsibilities included the upkeep of the appliances and weekly tests on the street alarms and call bells.

He was conscious of these responsibilities in a town whose population more than doubled in the holiday season. He felt the need for a quicker response, and so urged the council to consider permanent horsing for the appliances.

The matter was debated at great length but in the end the council resolved that horses would be provided from the Corporation Works Department in Lake Road, more than half a mile from the station. This hardly represented an improvement on existing arrangements.

To overcome the inevitable delay in turn-out time, the brigade had developed the practice of using a motor car from the Athol Garage, which was close to the station, and sending four or five men to a fire, ahead of the appliances (as in the case of the Laxey Glen Pavilion blaze). Very often these men had extinguished the fire before the arrival of the horse-drawn pumps.

A fire requiring major pumping facilities outside the town limits was an even bigger problem, as the brigade again found at Laxey in January 1921 when fire broke out at J Corlett's flour mill.

The fire started shortly after noon and developed amazingly quickly. The company clerk, George Quayle, had to leave without the books or the contents of the safe. Men had to run from the building as the fire spread up the natural flues provided by the wooden grain chutes which passed between the floors.

There was modern fire-fighting equipment on the premises and workmen connected their hoses to hydrants fed from the cistern on top of the building. They made a brave attempt to fight the fire but were quickly beaten back by the heat.

The Laxey Fire Brigade, which had only recently been formed, was soon on the scene. However, it only had hose and branches, relying entirely on hydrant pressure. The men were powerless to do anything — the whole mill was on fire and the roof collapsed shortly after their arrival, sending flames higher than the mill chimney.

At 1pm word was sent to Douglas for urgent assistance. Mr Pickett obtained a car from the Athol Garage, throwing in several lengths of hose and other equipment before setting off with some of the brigade. They arrived within 20 minutes, by which time it was obvious that the mill could not be saved. They turned their attention to the burning roof of the adjoining screen house. Their efforts undoubtedly saved this building from destruction.

The Laxey men continued to play water on the main mill building until the steam fire engine arrived from Douglas. No time had been lost in procuring two horses, but it was 15 minutes before they were harnessed up and under way with six firemen. The horses were worked hard and it took one and a quarter hours to travel the seven hilly miles to Laxey.

They arrived at 2.30pm and raised steam in 20 minutes. There was some difficulty at first with the suction valve and there was a deep lift from the river. After a few minutes full suction was obtained and a considerable quantity of water was thrown on to the fire, which had by this time been burning for more than two hours. The engine was later moved to the rear of the mill and the firemen prevented the fire spreading to the engine house. The fire in the main building was brought under control shortly afterwards.

The roof and all the floors of the main building had collapsed, together with machinery. As men from the mill attempted to

The fire at the Laxey Flour Mills in 1921. The Laxey men are on the left of the picture. (Photograph: Manx Museum)

clear away the debris, smouldering timber continued to flare up. The Laxey brigade stayed in attendance damping down for 22 days.

The Laxey brigade had been formed on January 7, 1920 with Mr F B Holroyd as captain. Its equipment consisted of a small hose cart, acquired from J Blakeborough & Sons Ltd, of Brighouse, Yorkshire, and several lengths of hose, a standpipe and branches. All this equipment was kept beneath the Commissioners' office, which opened at the rear onto Lower Rencell Hill.

The Highways Committee of Douglas Corporation had meanwhile taken note of its brigade's earlier representations and considered specifications of motor appliances. After hearing Mr Pickett's views they recommended that a Leyland Motor Fire Combination, complete with all accessories, should be ordered

without delay. The 65hp Leyland arrived in January 1921. It carried a 500gpm pump with two deliveries and 4" suction. The unlaiden weight of the vehicle was 10 tons and it was mounted on solid tyres. A standard wooden Bayley 50ft wheeled escape was carried; among the ancillary equipment were two Proto breathing sets and a smoke helmet with hose and bellows.

The vehicle was the first motor-driven fire appliance on the Island. It was registered as MN 1233 and was lettered "Douglas Corporation Motor Fire Engine No 1" on each side. The whole vehicle was supplied for £1,897 10s.

Had this machine arrived three weeks earlier, the outcome of the Laxey Mill story might have been rather different.

The new motor appliance necessitated the re-appraisal of the whole brigade. A full report was submitted by Mr H A Bridge, the

Borough Surveyor. The result was the appointment of Mr W J Pickett as Superintendent, a position which had not been filled since Mr O'Hara's death.

A revised scale of charges was approved, fixing the rate for the new appliance at £5 5s per hour, plus £1 for each additional hour within the Borough. Outside the town the charge was £10 10s per hour, plus £1 per mile beyond a five-mile radius of Douglas, with the same charge of £1 for each additional hour. The retaining fees and other charges were also revised.

In March 1921 the brigade establishment comprised the Superintendent, Captain (second officer), Motorman and 16 men. In addition to the motor appliance, the brigade still had the steam fire engine, a hosecart, five large-wheeled escapes and a tower ladder.

Eleven members of the brigade were connected to the station by call bells, maintained by the Post Office Telephone Company. Seven street alarms were incorporated in the system, located at the Villiers, Broadway, Crescent, Rosemount, market, gas works and Douglas Bridge. The Borough Surveyor and the brigade were pressing for additional alarms at Murrays Road, Tennis Road, Victoria Road and Derby Castle.

There was a serious fire in Douglas on Monday, January 12, 1925, at George Wilding's Hardware and General Dealer, in Duke Street. It was discovered by a neighbour at about 7.45pm.

The fire was at first confined to a long cellar under the property and a number of hoses were brought into use. The premises were surrounded by other buildings and access was difficult. The brigade brought hoses into the rear of the property through adjoining premises.

Just when it appeared that the fire was under control, there was a flash-over; it broke through into the shop above and spread rapidly, despite the efforts of the brigade.

Police moved people out of their houses in nearby Muckles Gate and, after the roof collapsed, the firemen concentrated their efforts on preventing the fire spreading. By 10.30pm the building was gutted and all that could be done was to damp down the remains.

The well-equipped Douglas brigade continued to deal with out-of-town fires and was able to prevent major outbreaks developing. A fire at the Halfway House Hotel, Crosby, which started in a timber lintel in a rear lavatory, would almost certainly have resulted in a major blaze ten years previously, but the brigade arrived 20 minutes after the fire was discovered and quickly extinguished it.

In August 1928 fire was discovered again at the Laxey Glen Mills. The outbreak started on the third floor and the alarm was immediately raised. Many members of the Laxey Fire Brigade worked at the mill and they, together with Mr Thomas, the manager, got to work with a hose. They tried to confine the fire until the arrival of the Douglas Brigade, which had been sent for at the outset.

The fire suddenly broke out in the upper section, having travelled up an elevator, and set light to the rafters. The Douglas Brigade had not yet arrived and an urgent call to the station confirmed that it had left half an hour earlier.

The fire was now assuming serious proportions but the Laxey men stood their ground inside the building and continued to confine the fire.

The Douglas appliance eventually arrived, having been delayed with a broken valve spring in Onchan. The firemen went to work quickly with additional jets from their motor pump and soon brought the fire under control. The Douglas men stripped the roof and left the Laxey brigade to damp down and clear up.

Whenever the new motor fire engine was attending an out-of-town fire, only the old steamer was left to cover any subsequent calls in Douglas. The brigade was not satisfied with this arrangement; representations had been made on a number of occasions suggesting that the council should provide an additional motor appliance. This latest fire in Laxey served to underline the problem.

In September 1928, the Highway Committee recommended the council to buy a 14hp Bean fire tender and two 30-gallon chemical extinguishers at a cost of £550.

In 1929 the responsibility for the fire brigade was transferred to the Works Committee. Its first job was to recruit younger men for the brigade as many were over the retirement age specified in brigade rules. The Superintendent himself, Mr W J Pickett, was

Men of the Douglas Brigade pose for a special event with their 65 hp Leyland pump escape in Lord Street. The appliance, delivered in 1921, was described as a combination fire appliance; it carried a 50ft wooden Bayley escape and was fitted with a 500gpm pump. It had a single first-aid hose reel on top of the Braidwood-type body. Two of the firemen are wearing Proto breathing sets — see also inset — and Jim Sloane has on a Siemens smoke suit and is carrying a smoke helmet.

two years over the limit at the age of 67. He retired in March having held the position for eight years.

The committee appointed Mr S J Caugherty as his successor and Mr A J O'Hara became Captain. Stephen A Caugherty took over as brigade secretary.

The new tender arrived in June and Douglas was now in a much better position to answer calls for assistance outside the Borough. It was Laxey yet again which tested the brigade with a series of fires over a two-year period.

The largest was a fire discovered in the Manx Electric Railway Company's rolling stock shed on Saturday, April 5, 1930 at 10.40pm. It had been locked shortly after mid-day when the electric car bringing workmen back to Laxey from the Dhoon Quarry had been put away.

The captain of the Laxey Brigade realised on arrival that he had a major incident on his hands and immediately called for assistance from Douglas. The Laxey firemen had trouble finding the hydrant in the main road, because it had been covered with tar.

The shed, 240ft long and 36ft wide, was full of rolling stock. It had obviously been burning for some time before it was discovered. The hydrant pressure was poor and the efforts of the firemen were to little effect. Company employees rushed to the shed and tried to save the contents.

Due to the intense heat, only two trailer cars were saved and one, trailer No 60, was on fire as it was rolled out. Once the doors had been opened, the fire increased in intensity. It was almost 11.30pm when the Douglas brigade arrived with the Leyland appliance.

Water was scarce and the mains supply inadequate. The Douglas men dammed the river below the shed and pumped water up to the fire. By this time the shed was completely engulfed. The overhead electricity supply had been turned off for safety. The firemen still could not get near enough to be effective, even though they had three jets in operation from the Leyland, and the Laxey brigade still had a jet running from the mains. The fire was being fed by the timberwork of the cars and the galvanised iron sheeting of the shed was glowing white hot. The heat

shattered the glass rooflights, allowing flames to shoot high into the air.

Soon the houses backing onto the shed were threatened and timberwork around windows and eaves ignited from the radiated heat. The firemen had to leave the shed to burn itself out and concentrate on saving the houses and other nearby properties.

The Leyland pumped continuously for three hours and the brigade was still there at 6am. The Leyland returned to Douglas and four firemen were left on watch until the Manx Electric's breakdown gang arrived from Douglas at 9.30am.

All that was left was a twisted mass of metal. Four motor tramcars, seven trailers and works equipment were lost in the fire.

The following year saw a similar fire in Douglas, this time involving charabancs rather than trams. The fire broke out in W H Shimmin's garage on the Promenade. The garage was built between two blocks of boarding houses and behind the house occupied by the proprietor.

The alarm had been raised by PC Quayle who also woke Mr Shimmin. With the help of some early-rising visitors, they pulled out six charabancs and seven motor cars from a new garage which adjoined the burning building.

Captain O'Hara arrived on the Bean tender shortly before 7am. The garage at the rear was a sea of flames, but the fire was to some extent contained by a galvanised roof of steel sheet. The brigade hauled out a burning vehicle and extinguished the fire in the bodywork. The men then set to work on the fire in the garage, bringing it under control by 8.30am, and leaving the scene by 11am. Five cars and two motorcycles were destroyed.

In June 1933 Douglas brigade had a full turn-out to a fire in Walpole Avenue at Victoria House, a large boarding house. Passers-by saw flames coming from the roof and raised the alarm. PCs Quine and Gelling were first on the scene, so they evacuated the building. They then attempted to check the fire from the top of the staircase using buckets of water.

The brigade arrived with the Bean tender, followed very shortly by the Leyland. Supt Caugherty and Capt O'Hara found the whole of the roof space above the attic bedrooms to be on fire.

The firemen set about tackling the blaze from below, working from the top landing.

The centre of the roof collapsed without warning and crashed down the stair well. The firemen had a narrow escape, but had to withdraw and extinguish the fire which had now broken out within the building.

The Bean was sent back to the station to tow the 65ft escape back to the scene. It was pitched with difficulty but the firemen could not use it because of the danger from falling slates. Eventually they got onto adjoining roofs and were able to tackle the fire from above, bringing it under control an hour and a half later.

This incident illustrated the problems facing the brigade when tackling fires in buildings more than four storeys high. The Superintendent made strong representation to the committee and, in due course, consideration was given to the provision of further equipment, including a turntable ladder.

After visits to various towns in England, and to Merryweather & Sons to view fire-fighting equipment, an order for three appliances was placed in August 1935.

The first was a 100ft Merryweather turntable fire escape on a purpose-built chassis powered by a 115hp six-cylinder Dorman engine, complete with an integral two-stage turbine pump delivering 500gpm at low pressure and 300gpm at high pressure. A monitor nozzle for the head of the ladder, telephones, searchlight and electric siren were all included in the quoted price of £3,565.

The second was a 90hp Merryweather petrol motor fire engine on an Albion chassis, complete with a Hatfield reciprocating pump rated at 400gpm. A 40-gallon water tank and first aid reel with 120ft of hose was included, together with a 45ft extension ladder. The appliance also carried a patent foam generator worked off the engine exhaust. The whole lot was quoted at £1,725.

The third item was a Merryweather Hatfield 22hp reciprocating trailer pump with a capacity of 165gpm. This appliance was the first to arrive, within weeks of the order being placed.

Douglas was expanding rapidly and there were attempts by the Borough to extend its boundaries, in particular by absorbing the village district of Onchan.

It was revealed by the committee of Tynwald, which had been set up to consider the proposals for extension of boundary, that the village had only limited fire-fighting cover from a volunteer brigade which had originally been formed in 1911 with Mr J T Skillicorn as the captain. The six members of the brigade had a handcart, hoses, ladders and small tools and their equipment was kept in Coupe's stables in Queens Road and, later, at the Commissioners' yard. The brigade had more recently received training from its Captain, Mr E Quiggin, and Mr Caugherty of the Douglas brigade.

At the time of the inquiry the Onchan Village Commissioners were considering the purchase of a fire engine, but for any major fire their reliance was still almost entirely on Douglas.

The new Douglas appliance arrived in April 1936. The turntable ladder was driven on a trial run through Onchan to the Liverpool Arms Hotel and back. The Albion was taken on a similar run to St John's. On April 6 a demonstration of the new vehicles was staged for the Works Committee at the Villiers Hotel; further demonstrations were held at Peel, Port Erin and the Ballamona Mental Hospital.

These demonstrations, at most of the Island's tall buildings, culminated in a grand display of fire-fighting staged jointly by Merryweather and Sons and Douglas Corporation, in Peveril Square, which included the four motor-driven appliances, the steamer and the hose cart.

Death on duty

The dubious distinction of becoming the first Island fireman killed in the course of his duty befell Robert Kenna on September 6, 1938.

Shortly after 12.45pm the brigade was called to Brown's menswear shop on North Quay. The Albion was dispatched with 15 men under the direction of Chief Officer Stephen Caugherty. The shop was well alight and the manager informed the brigade that the fire had started in the basement and that they had made an unsuccessful attempt to extinguish it before the alarm was raised.

When the first hose was played on the fire the firemen immediately told the chief that they had felt an electric shock. He then entered the building and tripped all the electrical switches that the manager knew about. Caugherty himself and another fireman felt further electrical shocks and he ordered the water to be cut off and the first floor floorboards to be lifted to get to the main electrical intake.

Fireman Kenna, who was on the first floor, walked over towards a window and stumbled on some debris. He reached out and caught hold of a hanging wire and let out a cry. Caugherty was behind him and, quickly realising what had happened, pulled the sleeves of his tunic over his hands and pulled Kenna away by the shoulders. Sadly, the fireman was already dead.

Following the inquest, various recommendations were made to the electrical undertakers concerning the placing of firemen's switches in accessible places in both public and domestic buildings.

Ramsey reorganisation

Meanwhile, in 1916, the Ramsey brigade was still operating its hose cart, manual engine and 60ft wheeled escape under the control of the Stables and Stores Committee. The first effect of the new legislation was a complete reorganisation at Ramsey, with new annual retaining fees and charges. A new rule book outlined the duties of the officers and members and it became effective from July 1, 1918.

During all this activity the brigade's Superintendent and longest serving member retired and the duties of the various officers were redefined. Branch-pipe men were set apart and given additional responsibilities, as was the turn-cock. To qualify for the annual retaining fee, the men were required to attend ten practices each year.

By 1928, the brigade's call-out time was slightly longer than before the turn of the century: nevertheless it was still efficient. The appliances were, however, becoming obsolete and the Commissioners resolved in August to buy a motor-driven appliance. A petition was presented to the Local Government Board for permission to borrow £1,000.

The new appliance was registered on September 20, 1928. It was a 30hp petrol-engined Merryweather Hatfield with a Braidwood body and a 400gpm pump.

It was formally handed over six days later to J N Richdale, chairman of the Commissioners, and a demonstration was held at Albert Road school under the direction of Mr F W Frear of Merryweather & Company. Water was thrown to a height of 180ft on the smallest jet and a delivery pressure of 140lbs psi was a tremendous improvement on hydrant pressure in the town mains which averaged a mere 40lbs psi.

The brigade strength was increased by three to 19 and Robert Cain was appointed driver of the motor engine. In November, at the request of the brigade members, the Town Commissioners agreed to name the new appliance *Richdale*.

The Commissioners informed the Local Government Board that they were now in a position to allow their brigade to attend fires outside the town boundary without restriction.

The manual engine, now obsolete, was offered for sale the following year. The call-bell system operated by the telephone company was also obsolete, and consideration was being given for its replacement or for the installation of a Smith's Patent Fire Alarm of the siren type.

All was not well with the *Richdale*. The brigade had experienced difficulty climbing some of the steep hills in the Mayhill and Ballure areas of the town. The matter was taken up with Merryweather's, who solved the problem at the company's own expense by changing the rear chain-drive sprockets from 17 to 14 teeth. This solved the hill climbing problem — but only at the expense of its top speed.

Lacking at Laxey

Following the fire at the Manx Electric Railway shed at Laxey, there had been some comment about the efficiency of the village brigade. A public meeting was held and the outcome was a re-organised brigade of 20 men, with the Commissioners appointing Mr D Williamson as Superintendent on June 4, 1930. Mr J Beck was appointed his deputy and brigade instructor.

Ramsey Fire Brigade pictured outside the Town Hall with the new Merryweather 30hp appliance, Richdale, the first motorised fire engine on the Island. Mr J Smith, the brigade's chief officer, is in the front row.

This picture shows the Douglas Brigade the following year, 1929, on the delivery of the 14hp Bean motor tender to the fire station in Lord Street. In the centre, sporting a moustache, is the brigade's superintendent, S J Caugherty, while on his right is the captain, A J O'Hara.

Almost two years later, in April, 1932, a bus employee noticed the Dhoon Glen Hotel on fire; he raised the alarm when he got to Laxey.

Williamson summoned the brigade at 7.45pm and had his men ready within six minutes. Although the hotel was outside their area they decided to respond to the call. They obtained Mr Faragher's van and set off. The Ramsey brigade had also been called out.

The Laxey Brigade got there first, but could do very little with its equipment. The Hotel, 40 years old and built of pitch pine, was completely engulfed in flames. The Ramsey men arrived soon afterwards and set up their motor pump by the river some distance away. Both brigades set about fighting the fire, although their work was hampered by the presence of a 300 gallon petrol tank in front of the hotel.

The road had to be closed after the building collapsed; burning embers flew across the entrance to the glen, threatening the trees. The licensee and his wife returned home at 10pm to find nothing left.

As the Ramsey brigade became more familiar with the new appliance, it was apparent that the brigade strength could be reduced and, on the recommendation of the Chief Officer, Mr J Smith, it was brought down by five, to 14.

At this time the Ramsey brigade was called to a fire in the town at a bakehouse belonging to Mrs W L Corlett, of Wattleworth's Café. The blaze was discovered by Harry Martin whose father had a grocery warehouse adjoining the bakehouse. On the other side of the bakehouse was a large grain warehouse. The fire was difficult to get to and potentially dangerous.

A large crowd had gathered in the early evening and saw William Corlett drive the engine at speed round the corner of East Street with the brigade holding on to the grab rails on the open body. The firemen arrived within five minutes of receiving the call: a remarkably quick turn-out. The fire was effectively dealt with and confined, though not without difficulty, to the bakehouse.

The motor driven appliance was still giving cause for concern, and Merryweather's sent a mechanic to inspect it. He reported that the crankcase was cracked and that there was also a bad crack in the cylinder bore which would necessitate the engine being returned to England for repair. He found the clutch and brakes worn and defective, though the pump was in good order.

Merryweather's was invited to quote for three alternative solutions to the problem. These were the replacement of the defective engine, its repair, or the replacement of the appliance utilising the old pump. In the meantime the Commissioners sent a deputation to Douglas to enquire from the Local Government Board when the new fire tender and trailer pump would be supplied to them under the proposed co-ordinated fire-fighting scheme. To some extent they were anticipating the forthcoming Local Government (Fires) Act, but their position left them with no alternative.

They bought a new 25hp Merryweather Automobile Fire Tender based on a Morris two-ton short wheelbase chassis, fitted with a 45ft extension ladder and first-aid reel, at a cost of £575. A Hatfield trailer pump had been ordered; it arrived the same month at a cost of £460.

Kirk Michael Commissioners did not form a fire brigade until 1933, although Government Office had reminded them of their obligations on a number of occasions since 1919.

They were preoccupied with installing a drainage system in 1925, and this was followed by involvement in a water supply system which was not completed until 1932. On May 27, 1931, however, the Commissioners did resolve to buy some fire extinguishing apparatus at a cost of £25 and an application was made to the Local Government Board for the necessary borrowing powers.

It was to be two years before a fire brigade was formed, with Mr F W Cowin as its Superintendent and Mr R S Quayle as his assistant, their appointments taking effect from September 9, 1933.

5. War threatens

The Local Government (Fires) Act, 1940

WITH THE THREAT of war looming, the UK Parliament was taking precautions which included the Fire Brigades Act of 1938. This gave the Government powers to take over areas not providing adequate means of fire-fighting and to co-ordinate the whole fire service if the need arose.

The Isle of Man was taking its own precautions and in May 1938 a Central Air Raids Precautions Committee was appointed under the chairmanship of Deemster Farrant.

The committee investigated all aspects of training for air raid wardens, police, fire and local authorities and submitted its report to Tynwald in November. Recommendations were made to increase the number of fire-fighting personnel and to provide more equipment. Early in 1939 came their final report which recommended the setting up of a district ARP organisation and made reference to the Local Government Board report on the all-Island scheme to co-ordinate the fire service.

This heralded the first reading of the Local Government (Fires) Bill in May 1939, which outlined requirements for the various districts, standardising equipment and making special provision for the Douglas Fire Brigade to operate over the whole Island.

Douglas Corporation was concerned that, having spent £6,979 on new appliances between 1935 and 1937 (plus the £2,725 a year it took to run the brigade), it was not going to get sufficient financial aid from the proposed legislation. It was worried enough to engage counsel, Edwyn Kneen, to represent it at the bar of the legislative chamber. The Act was passed in October and became law in February 1940, but already the war was six months old.

The Act defined seven fire authorities — Douglas, Ramsey, Castletown, Peel, Laxey, Michael and Rushen — with the Council and Local Commissioners administering all but the Rushen area, which was to continue under the control of the Rushen Joint Fire Protection Board, appointed in November 1938. It also specified that there should be mutual assistance between the various authorities.

A fire fund was raised from a penny rate and administered by the Local Government Board. Douglas and Ramsey were to receive set grants of £550 and £120 per annum respectively; the other areas had to keep accounts and submit annual estimates, together with applications for grant aid. Onchan Village Commissioners were the only exception, being covered under the Douglas Fire Authority Area, and were required to pay the Douglas Corporation £100 per annum towards the cost of maintaining their brigade.

The Island Government set up a War Emergency Committee in August 1939, directly responsible to the Governor. This was reconstituted the following November as the War Committee of Tynwald, under the chairmanship of Deemster W P Cowley. It dealt with all the problems of the war, in an executive capacity, until November 1945.

As in World War I, the Island was commandeered for the internment of aliens. Most hotels and boarding houses were used for this purpose, or for the billeting and training of military personnel. Soon the Island would be packed to capacity: a daunting prospect for its fire brigade whose deficiencies had been recognised in the Act.

Ramsey and the Rushen Joint Fire Protection Board had ordered new appliances in anticipation of the Act. During November 1939 Ramsey took delivery of a 24hp Merryweather appliance with a Braidwood type body built on a Morris chassis.

It came complete with a Coventry Climax trailer pump. The Ramsey Commissioners also bought an additional 25 hp Merryweather appliance in March 1940, at a cost of £870.

The Act proved effective in its first year: two motor fire tenders and five trailer pumps were distributed, with their cost defrayed by Insular Revenue.

In August 1940 Mr A R Corlett OBE was appointed Inspector of Equipment; he had previously been chief officer of the Manchester Fire Brigade. His new brief was to visit the Island twice a year to inspect all the equipment, and prepare reports on the state of the various brigades for consideration by the Board.

An Auxiliary Fire Services Scheme was introduced during the year at the request of the War Committee of Tynwald. It was prepared by the Chief Constable and the Chief Officer of the Douglas Fire Brigade under the direction of the Local Government Board. The long list of fire-fighting equipment was approved, with £6,018 being made available from Central Government to set up an Auxiliary Fire Service.

The Civil Defence Commission recommended that the Local Government Board chief inspector, Mr W E Quayle, should oversee the training of all the fire brigades and auxiliary fire forces. With the co-operation of the Chief Officer of the Douglas brigade, a suitable training programme was formulated.

Internment camps and military training units occupied the whole of the Douglas promenade and the central area of the town as well as part of Onchan. In July, Douglas brigade had its first call to one of these camps. At the Central Internment Camp it first experienced security problems with prisoners, which made fire-fighting even more difficult.

The Island learned many lessons from its first air raid warning, at 2.50pm on July 31, 1940. No central fire control or Auxiliary Fire Service stations had yet been established and, had the raid materialised, the Island would have been found wanting.

Meanwhile, Douglas brigade dealt with fires at the Palace, Hutchinson Square and Sefton Internment Camps. The fire at the 'Hydro' in the Palace Camp proved the most serious, requiring the attendance of Douglas No 2 and No 4 appliances.

On August 9, 1940 the first AFS practice was arranged, and 21 members of the AFS turned out with the Douglas Brigade. Subsequently there were several drills each week. The war dictated many such changes. Onchan Village Commissioners surrendered their equipment to Douglas on September 23 and effectively ceased to operate as a village brigade. In reality the members of the brigade joined the AFS and continued to function, training regularly with the Douglas Brigade and the Bean tender.

During February 1941 fire posts were established at Corlett Sons & Cowley's warehouse, Greeba Works in Market Street, McKibbin's Yard in Circular Road, Crown Bakery in Woodbourne Lane, the Corporation Bus Depot on York Road, the Corporation Deck Chair Store at the Esplanade, Pulrose Manor, Emmett's Garage on Woodside Terrace and Clifton House, St Ninian's.

Local tradesmen provided lorries, which were supplied with special badges. With the addition of Onchan, Strang and Crosby, a total of 12 fire posts had been established in the Douglas Fire Authority area by the end of the year. These posts were fully equipped and all personnel, both regular and auxiliary, were issued with steel helmets. Military guards at the various camps trained regularly with the AFS and part-time firemen.

Continuing the modernisation directed by the new Act, Douglas, Castletown and Peel acquired new appliances. Douglas took delivery of a 30hp Fordson towing vehicle and trailer pump on June 14, 1941. The appliance had an open body with locker space and a closed forward control cab. This released the Bean, dating from 1929, which was sold to the Castletown Commissioners.

At the outbreak of war Peel still only had its horse-drawn manual fire engine and hand-cart. Large areas of the town had been commandeered for use as internment camps, and the need for a modern fire appliance was urgent. The Commissioners ordered a 20hp Commer fire tender with an open Braidwood-type body and a Merryweather Hatfield trailer pump. They arrived on September 19 and gave Peel a fire-fighting capability, although still falling short of what was considered desirable.

During the year the need for a Central Control and the establishment of a Chief Fire Staff Officer became more urgent. The Local Government Board consulted the Chief Fire Advisor to the Home Office and appointed, on his recommendation, Mr C A P Ellis as Chief Fire Staff Officer. He attended his first drill on May 10, 1942, his skill and enthusiasm soon winning respect from the local brigades.

In the same month, the first of four Austin standard Home Office pattern Auxiliary Towing Vehicles arrived. They were fitted with 35ft extension ladders and 500gpm trailer pumps. These vehicles were obtained by the Manx Government and issued to the Douglas area.

By February 1943 ten of these standard towing vehicles had been supplied. In addition to the four supplied to Douglas, two were allocated to Castletown and one each to Ramsey, Peel, Rushen and Laxey. Auxiliary Fire Stations were built in Laxey, Ballasalla, Andreas, Foxdale and Kirk Michael.

Training was stepped up to familiarise the crews with the ATVs, and included crews from *HMS Valkyrie* and the RAF which operated similar equipment. Douglas brigade provided training in the use of escapes and ladders on the practice tower in Lord Street's public car park, using the Merryweather turntable ladder, the Bayley wheeled escape and the Telescale escape ladder.

Large-scale exercises were centred on static water tanks placed strategically around Douglas, giving the AFS good experience in the use of their trailer pumps. On one occasion an all-Island exercise was staged on the assumption that Douglas had received a major air attack and that the mains water supply had been severed. The whole of the Douglas and out-of-town AFS were involved in pumping water by relay from Port-e-Chee and the River Glass to the static tank at Waverly Terrace using the small Coventry Climax pumps. The larger Hatfield trailer pumps provided a further relay to the Derby Square static tank.

The exercise proved that the fire service could respond if the Island were to suffer a genuine air-raid, and draw water for several miles if necessary.

In February 1940 a fire broke out about 7am at Knottfield in Woodbourne Road. Neighbours were awakened by the screams of servants from the rear of the house and the alarm was raised. Albert Rowell, the owner of the house, received burns rescuing the three maid servants, but all the occupants escaped safely.

When the Douglas Brigade arrived, a few minutes later, flames were shooting through the roof at the rear of the mansion. Several members of the brigade escaped serious injury when a gas explosion ripped through the house and engulfed the main staircase. The roof quickly became a mass of flames and, despite water being directed onto the building from the turntable ladder, the house could not be saved. The brigade returned to station 11 hours later.

Black-out

Because of the air-raid precautions, and the need to fulfil black-out regulations, it was essential that farm and heath fires were extinguished without delay. At 7.10pm on Saturday, October 24, 1942, Peel Brigade was called out for a fire at Ballanayre Farm, north of the town. Fifteen minutes later the brigade left Peel, with the new Commer fire tender towing the Hatfield pump.

When the men arrived they found all the farm buildings on fire. The police had sent word to Douglas requesting assistance, but the situation was already desperate.

The nearest water supply was a quarter of a mile away. The trailer pump was got to the stream with difficulty and, by 8pm, three jets were playing on the fire. Douglas brigade arrived soon afterwards, with its Fordson tender, Hatfield trailer pump and 14 men. They put their pump into the same stream, but found there was not enough water to supply both pumps. Douglas shut theirs down, but stayed at the scene to relieve the Peel men by taking alternate spells at fighting the fire. They eventually returned to station at 1.30am on Sunday, when the fire had been brought under control.

Peel brigade stayed at the farm until 5am when the fire was out, leaving a watchman until 8am. The buildings were gutted and many tons of hay were lost.

During October, Peel also took delivery of an Austin towing vehicle and trailer pump.

At the end of the month there was an early morning call to a fire at 11 Beach Street. The occupant was Captain Wallace, a member of the Women's Royal Army Corps, who was woken by choking smoke. She tried to fight her way downstairs, but was beaten back by the fire and smoke. In desperation she smashed the window, jumped some ten feet into the street and ran to the police station to raise the alarm.

The Commer arrived with eight men, who were soon fighting the fierce blaze. However, as the flames were being brought under control it became apparent that the fire was being fed by a gas-pipe burning free under the stairs.

The fire had melted a lead pipe, making it essential that the gas supply be turned off. Fireman Bell, later to become Captain of the brigade, crawled into the burning building, located the incoming supply pipe and turned off the gas. The lower storey of the building was completely gutted, and the remainder severely damaged.

The Peel area had by this time established an Auxiliary Fire Service with fully equipped posts. A number of full-scale exercises were held in Peel, confirming that in a real emergency the whole town could be covered using water from the harbour by relay pumping, with four light pumps and five heavy ones.

Peel also exercised regularly with Kirk Michael and Ramsey brigades, and on one occasion with RAF Jurby for familiarisation with aircraft fires.

During the war a wheeled escape was stationed in Stanley Road, in full view of the many aliens interned in houses over two storeys high. Its demise was hastened by being stored outdoors; in 1946 it went for scrap. This was probably one of the old Douglas street escapes.

Heath fires rage

Perhaps the worst heath fire of the war broke out during May, 1943, on South Barrule. The glow could be seen in Douglas and Mr Ellis, on duty at Central Control in John Street, despatched the Fordson tender and trailer pump before the call for assistance came from the Peel Brigade. The ATV and pump from No 2 firepost were sent soon afterwards. Peel and Castletown brigades turned out with their appliances, and a full complement of men from the Foxdale fire-post were picked up by the Douglas ATV.

The Foxdale fire-post did not receive its ATV until the end of June.

On arrival at Barrule the men found no water supply, so they fought the fire with beaters and hand extinguishers. The whole operation was directed from the Central Fire Control which had been established in the basement of the Douglas fire station in John Street. The telephones and switchgear were manned by women members of the AFS, of whom 16 were trained for control room duty.

The Douglas fire-posts were manned by 71 members of the AFS. Drills and practices continued on a regular basis, particular emphasis being put on the Central Mobilising Scheme which involved units from all the fire authority areas.

The same year a number of standard Home Office canvas dams were supplied to supplement the static tanks. The four ATVs at Douglas were strategically placed to cover the town. FMN 237 was attached to No 1 fire-post, but garaged at E B Christian's garage. Similarly, FMN 280 was attached to No 2 firepost, but kept in Fayle's garage on Well Road Hill. FMN 238 was garaged at the firepost in Woodbourne Lane, with FMN 248 at firepost No 10 in the Onchan Commissioners' Yard.

The Royal Navy operated an ATV and trailer pump from a converted shop in Shore Road at the bottom of Broadway. It also had a Gwynne Major pump which was lorry-mounted on a standard wartime chassis; this was stationed in a converted seaside shelter on the Loch Promenade opposite the Royal Navy shore station, *HMS Valkyrie*.

Fire-fighting teams were attached to other military establishments in the town. The Signals Camp near the Palace had a team of women who regularly drilled with a trailer pump. There were teams at the Officer Cadet Training Unit stationed at the Villiers, *HMS St George*, and even a team of aliens at the Port Jack Internment Camp. All these units trained regularly throughout the war with the Douglas Brigade.

Fire watching was carried by volunteers from the Loyal Manx Association, which later assumed full Home Guard duties. Some of the larger departmental stores in Douglas also maintained fire-watching teams.

Under the provisions of the new Act, the Local Government Board allocated a motor tender and trailer pump to Laxey. The appliance was based on a Dodge van which had been converted to a fire tender by Ashton's Garage in Westmoreland Road in Douglas.

The vehicle was registered in the Laxey Village Commissioners' name in November 1940; by December 4 it had been delivered by Mr Caugherty and undergone tests in the area. The Laxey brigade was not satisfied with the performance of the tender, and returned it to Douglas for modifications.

The fire station under the Commissioners' Office was extended to accommodate it, but the new tender was never successful as a brigade appliance. It lacked power on the steep hills around Laxey, and it was returned to the Local Government Board within a year, to be reallocated to the Harbour Board.

The Commissioners preferred to use A R Caine's lorry until they took delivery of an Austin ATV in May 1942. In July the brigade establishment was fixed at 11 men. The Laxey Fire Authority set up an Auxiliary Fire Service with an establishment of 25 men, with fireposts in Laxey and Garwick, all under the direct control of Mr Williamson. On March 6, 1943 the alarm was raised to a fire at Ballaragh farm, high above Laxey with no mains water available.

The Laxey Brigade arrived shortly after midnight to find the farm buildings well alight. David Williamson lost no time in calling for assistance from the Douglas Brigade, and at 12.40am the ATV and trailer pump left No 1 firepost. This was followed shortly after by the Fordson tender towing the Hatfield trailer pump. The firepost at Onchan was alerted and its men left for Laxey with their ATV and pump.

The nearest water supply was over a mile way at Gretch Vooar. The firemen set about damming the stream, then relayed the water more than 7,000ft to the fire using three major pumps and two light trailer pumps.

Late on a Friday afternoon in July 1944, PC Godfrey, who was outside the police station at Laxey, became aware of the high-pitched note of an aircraft engine. Looking up he saw a plane on fire, diving out of control over the village. It disappeared over South Cape; almost immediately there was an explosion and a pall of smoke. PC Godfrey called the fire brigade and set off to the scene of the crash. Wreckage was strewn over a two-mile radius on the Grawe farm; the crew of nine all perished.

Part of the wreckage fell on a house at Fairy Cottage and set it on fire. A young child was killed and the other occupants all received burns. First on the scene were three members of the South Cape AFS post, who rescued the five people from the house and were fighting the fire by the time the brigade arrived from the village.

The Laxey brigade was the only one on the Island to be called by a maroon (flare). This procedure was discontinued during the war; afterwards Laxey fell into line with other towns and villages and used an air-raid siren. David Williamson resigned as chief officer of the brigade in 1947, and Mr W J Bridson succeeded him.

The Kirk Michael brigade was by this time operating as an efficient unit. However, it had started out at the beginning of the war with the minimum of equipment and a handcart kept in a lean-to shed at the rear of the Commissioners' offices. The brigade had been summoned as required by word of mouth.

The Water and Stores Committee had drawn up new rules for the brigade, which were approved in June 1940. The following month a full ARP was put into operation in Kirk Michael and an Auxiliary Fire Service formed. Mr S Keig was appointed Superintendent of the AFS, with Mr L Lowe as his deputy. Fireposts were established and stirrup pumps issued; the first practice was called for July 26.

On their way back from keeping watch on the hill above the village on August 3, members of the Local Volunteer Defence Corps saw flames coming from a shed in Kelly Brothers' yard. They raised the alarm in the village; by 5.30am the brigade was at the scene and soon had water on the fire. Ramsey brigade arrived after 6am. The two brigades had the fire under control by 9am and by noon it was out. Damage was considerable, with most of the buildings and engineering plant destroyed.

In November the Commissioners agreed on a five-year lease of J D Kelly's premises in Main Road for its fire station. Alterations were completed by February.

During 1941 Mr F W Cowin retired as the brigade's superintendent and was succeeded by PC G W A Kinrade, as Chief Officer. In February 1942 Mr Ellis delivered a Gwynne trailer pump to Kirk Michael, giving the brigade its first mechanical pump.

In June the Commissioners purchased the Bean tender from Castletown; it was the village's first motorised appliance. It would not fit in the existing fire station, so was housed in Quayle's Garage until a new fire station could be built next to the Mitre Hotel. Edmund Quayle was appointed brigade mechanic and put in charge of the appliance.

Early in 1943 the new station was completed and the motor tender and pump installed. The Bean was replaced in April 1946 by a 20hp Austin towing vehicle acquired from the Peel Commissioners. It was used with the Coventry Climax trailer pump which had been previously used by the Kirk Michael AFS, the Gwynne pump having been loaned to the Sulby AFS firepost.

Changes in the north

Ramsey had been well equipped at the outbreak of war and trained regularly under the direction of Chief Officer Mr J Smith. The brigade used the Longworth escape on the new pump escape carrier; the old Shand Mason escape was put in store. It did not stay there long, however, once the North Promenade houses had been requisitioned to form the Mooragh Internment Camp. Painted and repaired, it became operational again, being stationed in the Commissioners' Yard at the Mooragh. The brigade took delivery of an *X-aust* suds generator at the same time, to give it a foam-making capability.

In 1941 the brigade strength was increased to 20, and the AFS establishment stayed at the same figure. Fireposts were established in the Ramsey area, as elsewhere, and supplied with manual pumps, although the Sulby post had a major pump at a later date. In June 1942 one of the Austin ATVs and a trailer pump were allocated to Ramsey, being temporarily housed in the railway station yard.

The war saw the building of military aerodromes at Jurby and Andreas; suddenly the remote country areas to the north of the Island came alive with personnel, aircraft and fuel stores with their attendant fire risks.

Andreas village and the new RAF training station came within the Ramsey Fire Authority Area, and Chief Officer Smith of the Ramsey brigade visited the aerodrome at the request of the Station Fire Prevention Officer during January 1942. He found that the military hydrants, standpipes and couplings were of a different pattern to those used elsewhere on the Island. The only help that the brigade could offer in the event of a fire was skilled personnel.

An auxiliary fire-post was established in the Andreas village. During 1943 one of the five new stations being built in the Island was commissioned there and the Ramsey ATV and trailer pump transferred.

A similar situation had existed within the Castletown Area, and another of the new fire stations was built in Ballasalla with an ATV and trailer pump being transferred from Castletown.

There were also military establishments within the Peel Fire Authority Area; in addition to the fireposts in the town at Market Place, Peveril Road and Stanley Road, there were remote posts at St John's, Foxdale and Glenmaye.

The presence of an RAF radio station at Dalby and a camp with living quarters at Glenmaye made it a vulnerable area, particularly as water was always scarce. A static tank was built on the station with a 6,000 gallon capacity and a Service trailer pump was provided. The captain of the Peel Brigade undertook the training of the service personnel, together with the members of the AFS from the Glenmaye firepost who operated a light trailer pump.

On June 21, 1943 another of the five new stations was completed at the Foxdale firepost; shortly afterwards the ATV and Gwynne trailer pump were transferred from Peel.

The Peel area had to deal with most of the heath fires during the war. Each one had to extinguished, often under extremely difficult conditions, because of the stringent emergency regulations. Unfortunately, agricultural land could not be insured against fire damage, which meant that the Authority could make

Peel brigade with the new 20hp Commer fire tender, delivered in 1941. The tender usually towed a Merryweather Hatfield trailer pump, as it was not normally fitted with one itself. All hose, standpipes, branches and other equipment were carried in lockers on the tender and the men rode on the open bodywork.

no claim for its services and the firemen did not get paid.

Understandably, loyalty was stretched almost to the point of rebellion. Eventually, after representation was made by their chief officer, the men received ten shillings each for attending heath fires.

Castletown was ill-equipped at the outbreak of war, with just the disused manual engine and a ladder cart. The brigade had only one fire call between 1934 and 1940, but the influx of military personnel billeted in the town soon changed that and during the next three years there were 11 calls.

As a result of the new Act, Castletown Commissioners ad-ministered the Castletown Fire Area, forming a Fire Fighting Executive sub-committee for the purpose. They set about reorganising the brigade yet again. New regulations were drawn up by September 1940, the old brigade was disbanded and a new one came into being. T Corkill remained as Captain of the retained brigade and at the same time an Auxiliary Fire Service was formed.

In July 1941 the Bean motor tender was purchased from Douglas for £100, so the town got its first motor-driven fire appliance. A Merryweather Hatfield trailer pump was acquired and the brigade was able to function as a reasonably efficient unit.

The following year an Austin ATV, FMN 259, was allocated to Castletown and the Bean sold to Kirk Michael Fire Authority. In February 1943 a second Austin ATV and light trailer pump were stationed at Castletown until the fire station at the Ballasalla firepost could be built, after which they was transferred to provide cover for the military establishments in the area.

AFS posts were established within the Castletown area at Ballasalla, Colby, Ballabeg and St Mark's, with Derbyhaven following later. All the posts were supplied with two-man manual pumps except for Ballasalla which had the ATV, FMN 451, and pump, and Ballabeg which had a four-man manual pump.

Mr D C McGowan was appointed leading fireman in the AFS. Monthly drills were supervised by the Captain of the regular brigade assisted by Sub-Captain J W Oates. In 1942 Mr Ellis undertook much of the training, achieving a high degree of efficiency with the limited equipment available.

Thomas Corkill resigned in May 1942, and J W Oates was appointed Captain of the Brigade. F L Kennaugh filled the post of Sub-Captain until 1944 when he in turn became Captain.

During 1943 a total of 29 men from the Castletown area were engaged over a period of several days fighting heath fires on South Barrule. The question of pay for attending such fires was now raised by Castletown, eventually resulting in the same fee as had been agreed at Peel. It was fortunate that the matter was resolved because they fought another heath fire on Barrule in March 1944, the men being engaged for days with beaters owing to the lack of water and water tenders.

Major Young, the ARP Controller, wrote to Port Erin Commissioners in September 1940, reminding them of their obligation to establish an AFS to participate in the Island's ARP fire-fighting scheme. They wrote back to say that the matter was being dealt with by the Rushen Joint Protection Board.

The Rushen Brigade had an establishment of ten men; eight were stationed at Port Erin under PC Cowin and two at Port St Mary with John Hyslop in charge. The new Merryweather motor appliance and trailer pump, which had been ordered earlier, arrived at Douglas late in 1939. Built on a 25hp Morris chassis, it carried a 50ft wartime version of the Bayley escape.

Mr S A Caugherty, chief officer of the Douglas Brigade, delivered it to Port Erin and undertook to train the Rushen Brigade to use the new appliance which was housed at the premises in the Falcon's Nest Yard.

The requisitioning of the boarding houses and hotels in Port Erin and Port St Mary for internees soon found the area in need of additional fire-fighting equipment. In June 1942 an Austin towing and trailer pump was delivered to Rushen and allocated to Port St Mary. A shed in the Commissioners' Yard was converted to accommodate the new appliance. The hoses and equipment were transferred from the hand-cart which was then taken out of service. PC Cowin had been transferred to St John's in 1941; Mr J R Costain replaced him as Captain, a position he held until 1947.

During the war the Rushen Brigade trained regularly with Douglas and Peel Brigades and also participated in the all-Island relay pumping exercises. John Hyslop, who had been in charge of the Port St Mary sub-station since 1939, was appointed Captain of the Rushen brigade in 1947.

Difficulties had been experienced by the Local Government Board in carrying out some of the statutory requirements of the 1940 Act. To remedy this an amending bill was prepared and placed before the Legislative Council on November 2, 1943.

The Fire Brigades Act 1938 in the United Kingdom incorporated recommendations of the Riverdale Committee which had been appointed two years earlier by the Home Secretary. It consolidated and amended the law relating to fire brigades in England.

The Manx Act of 1940 set out to do the same thing. There were a number of differences, however; the principal one was that in the Isle of Man it remained the liability of the owner or occupier of a property to pay for the services of the brigade attending at a fire.

This point had come into contention in respect of fires on heaths and agricultural land where it was not the general practice to insure against fire. The amending bill attempted to solve some of these problems.

The bill received its third reading in November and then

passed to the House of Keys for its first reading in December. It had a stormy passage and at its second reading the Douglas Corporation was represented by counsel who objected to certain sections.

The whole matter was referred to a committee of the House of Keys under the chairmanship of James Clinton MHK; its report and recommendations were published on August 1, 1944.

On the same day, Peel brigade was called to a fire at Ballakilmurray farm. The Commer and Hatfield pump were dispatched shortly after 9.30am with three members of the brigade and three helpers; three more brigade members followed later by car. On arrival they found the stables burnt out and the roof collapsed. They confined the fire and had it extinguished by noon.

The Peel men had to contend with many farm fires but the difficulty of getting water, particularly at the last fire, prompted Robert Kneen, the Captain of the brigade, to write in his report: "I am concerned at the frequency of these farm fires and the shortage of water in every case, and the attention of Government Office might be drawn to this fact with the object of making it compulsory for all farms to provide a static water tank for use in case of fire." He was not alone; other brigades were voicing similar concerns.

There was another farm fire near Peel during January 1945, this time at Ballanayre farm. The brigade found that the stables, packed with straw, were well on fire. The men had the same problem with water and it was almost an hour before they were able to tackle the fire. The straw was packed so tight that the water had no effect; instead the bales had to be manhandled into the yard, turned over and extinguished in the open. It was six hours before the fire was put out.

The AFS ceased to function shortly after the end of the war, in 1945. The equipment was collected from the fire-posts and put into Central Fire Stores. All posts were closed down except for Foxdale, Andreas and Sulby. Six of the Austin ATVs were retained, eventually being stationed at Rushen, Laxey, Castletown, Douglas, Andreas and Foxdale. The other four were disposed of locally within a few months.

The War Committee of Tynwald recognised the valuable work that Mr Ellis had done during the emergency as Chief Fire Officer and suggested that his services be retained by transfer from the Civil Defence Commission to the Local Government Board. The following month he took up his duties as Inspector of Equipment under the Local Government (Fires) Act 1940.

In the United Kingdom the Fire Services Act 1947 had been introduced. Its main effect was to wind up the National Fire Service and abolish Municipal Borough Councils, Urban District Councils and Joint Fire Boards as Fire Authorities. It also laid down certain standards of attendance at fires in respect of appliances, time and personnel.

The Island's politicians considered the introduction of similar legislation, but what started out as a seemingly simple piece of legislation soon developed into something quite different.

Meanwhile, it was business as usual for the Island's brigades, although one incident in June 1947 was relevant to some of the arguments being raised by the legislators concerning boundaries of the various fire authorities and the need for a central fire control.

A fire was discovered in a cottage at Santon by the son of the family who lived there. He had just lit a fire in the hearth and walked out of the cottage to talk to a neighbour. They were soon both alarmed to see smoke coming from the building. The Douglas and Castletown police were notified immediately and they informed the Castletown Brigade.

Mr Kennaugh, Captain of the brigade, knew the property and that it was outside the Castletown Fire Authority Area. He told the police he would attend the fire if the Douglas Brigade were not prepared to do so, though he needed their permission.

A police constable and a sergeant left Castletown for the fire; meanwhile Douglas Brigade was unsure of the location of the property, or if it was in its area. The result was that neither fire brigade turned out; the fire raged unchecked and the cottage was gutted. This predicament was one faced by the owners of many such properties situated on the limits of adjacent fire authority areas. This, with the question of payment for services, was among questions addressed in the proposed legislation.

Four die

The following year, on August 27, a tragic fire occurred at a lodging house, at 2 Mona Terrace, in which four people lost their lives. It was the most serious fire recorded up to this time in the Island.

The fire had started in a back sitting room on the ground floor. The tenant, a 55-year-old widow, discovered the fire at about 5am. She smelled smoke and went downstairs to investigate. When she opened the door to the back room, the fire engulfed the staircase. Nevertheless, she was able to raise the alarm and warn the others in the house before she was overcome by smoke.

With the staircase ablaze, all the occupants were marooned on the upper floors. The woman's son made his escape to the property next door by edging along a narrow ledge on the front of the building. The husband of a couple living at the rear of the house jumped from a bedroom window some 24 feet into the back yard. He urged his wife to follow but was then unable to break her fall. She was taken to hospital by taxi but died later from her injuries.

The police were first on the scene, at 5.15am. As PC Curphey was getting a ladder from a nearby builders' yard, the fire brigade came, under the direction of Alfie O'Hara, the Chief Officer. A full crew of seven men had arrived at the station within four minutes of the call. They immediately set to work and by 6.45am the fire was under control. But two people had died in the fire in addition to the woman who jumped. The tenant died the following day from her injuries. These two events had a profound effect on the discussions which were taking place on the introduction of the new legislation.

6. Towards one service

The Local Government (Fire Services) Act, 1950

THE BILL which had been introduced to amend the 1940 Act got no further than its second reading. Debate had been heated and, as a result, the House of Keys appointed a committee to consider the Local Government (Fires) Act, 1944. The report was published in August 1944 but its recommendations were never acted upon.

In an attempt to resolve the matter a Fire Service Commission was appointed by the Governor under the chairmanship of Ramsey G Johnson. The Commission was instructed to consider the establishment of a single Insular Fire Brigade or, if this was found to be inadvisable, to recommend changes in the existing system. It deliberated for several years, eventually publishing its report in November 1948.

Not surprisingly, many of the issues raised in the now dormant Bill of 1944 came under review. The vexed question of the boundaries between adjacent fire authority areas was also very carefully considered.

The Commission eventually concluded that the Island should keep the existing system of fire brigades maintained by local authorities, but under the overall direction of the Local Government Board. It did, however, agree to the boundary alterations called for in the 1944 Bill and further recommended that Foxdale, which at the time of the inquiry fell within three fire authority areas, should be placed in one area. It also recommended the abolition of payment for the services of a fire brigade, subject to

The carefully posed picture on the facing page was taken in 1950 on the car park at Lord Street, Douglas, used by the brigade there for training. Pictured, from the left, are the Fordson towing vehicle, an Austin auxiliary towing vehicle and the Albion Merryweather major pump.

certain interim measures. Finally it was recommended that the Local Government Board should appoint a Chief Fire Staff Officer.

As a result of the fire at 2 Mona Terrace, the Lt Governor also directed the Commission to inquire into the provision of means of escape in case of fire for people staying in boarding houses or hotels. Under existing legislation such buildings were only required to provide proper means of escape in case of fire if the height of the building exceeded 40ft. As 2 Mona Terrace was below this height, the provisions of the relevant Acts did not apply and no external fire escape had been provided.

The Commission recommended the introduction of legislation requiring all flats, tenements or public buildings exceeding two storeys to be provided with a proper means of internal or external escape. A Fire Escapes Bill succeeded at its initial presentation and became law in April 1950.

The Fire Escapes Act gave the Local Government Board wide powers to require owners and occupiers of certain buildings to provide proper means of escape in the case of fire and to impose penalties for non-compliance. It also made provision for loan advancement to enable owners of buildings to comply with the regulations.

In October 1951, before the regulations had been introduced, a disastrous fire completely gutted a shop and the flat above. The fire emphasised the importance of the Act and the need for an alternative means of escape in certain types of premises.

Shortly before 4am on Thursday, October 6, Walter Howarth, the proprietor of the Waterloo Hotel in Strand Street, was wakened by people shouting and the noise of breaking glass. He was told that the premises next door, above Hotchkis's shop, were on fire.

His wife telephoned the fire brigade at 3.55am, while he and his son-in-law tried to force an entry through the rear of the premises. They were joined by John Burns, a neighbour, who managed to climb onto an outhouse roof and rescue a 14-year-old girl who had been pushed through a window by her 21-year-old sister, Peggy. The fire beat the rescuers back, however, and Peggy and another younger sister died in the fire.

Having been unable to reach the children for the smoke and flames, their mother had managed to climb out of a first floor window at the front of the building. A policeman helped her down from the ledge above the shop front. A lodger in the house climbed from the window of his room on the same floor and then tried to pull himself up to the second floor window where he knew that Peggy was sleeping. He managed to pull himself up to the window ledge and break the glass, but he saw that the room was empty. She had gone to her sister's room at the rear of the house.

The fire brigade arrived, under the direction of Chief Officer Courtie, seven minutes after getting the call. This was an exceptionally good turn-out, but on arrival the men found the building completely engulfed by fire. While Fireman Quirk was laying on two jets, Mr Courtie learned that two people were unaccounted for. Two firemen wearing Proto sets entered the building, with little regard for their own safety, but they were too late.

The Fire Services Bill was presented in November 1949 and was eventually passed by Tynwald on January 31, 1950.

The Local Government (Fire Services) Act, 1950, became law on May 16th. As required by its provisions, the Local Government Board elected a Fire Services Committee with representation from each fire authority area. Each of the Local Authorities were designated as Fire Authorities, with the Rushen Joint Fire Protection Board restyled as the Rushen Fire Authority.

Douglas Fire Authority Area had been inspected twice a year, by Mr Ellis in his capacity as Inspector of Appliances, under the requirements of section 20 of the 1940 Act. During an inspection in November 1948 he noted that the Leyland pump escape was not at the station. Further investigation showed it had beeen loaned to the Isle of Man Airports Board on September 11 and was stationed at Ronaldsway Airport.

It was still absent at the next inspection, and Mr Ellis was concerned that Douglas was without a pump escape. In his report to the Local Government Board, he urged that it should be replaced.

Holiday properties

Douglas was the fire area with the most multi-storey properties, many of them used as boarding houses during the holiday season. The Douglas Brigade had the only turntable ladder on the Island, but now had no appliance, apart from the Albion with the Telescala ladder, carrying a wheeled escape. The loss of a major pumping unit was serious, but could be offset against the trailer pumps which were still available.

On February 22, 1950, the Works Committee of the Borough considered the provision of a new escape-carrying appliance, and a deputation led by Alderman J C Fargher went to Merryweather and Sons to inspect the latest types. Mr Ellis had by now left the Island, though he still acted as Inspector of Appliances. He arranged for an inspection and drill during April.

The Local Government Board was required under the terms of the new Act to appoint a Chief Fire Staff Officer, so they approached the Douglas Corporation to enquire if any officer they appointed could be seconded part-time to their brigade. A deputation from the Works Committee discussed the matter with the Board, but with five full-time firemen already employed by the Borough, it is not surprising that nothing came from the meeting.

Alfie O'Hara, Chief Officer of the Douglas Brigade, retired on April 1, 1950, having completed an impressive career. He had served 40 years as a voluntary fireman before being appointed full-time Second Officer in 1941 and Chief Officer in 1945. He was succeeded by Fred Courtie, and Bert Kenna was promoted from Sergeant to Second Officer.

The sub-committee returned from Merryweathers, made its recommendation to the Works Committee, and an official order

for a new pump escape was placed on May 5, 1950.

During July, Mr H M Smith, Chief Inspector of Fire Services to the Home Office, visited the Island to advise the Local Government Board on the selection of a Chief Fire Staff Officer. Mr S J Mayall was appointed early in 1951.

Late in March 1951 Douglas took delivery of its new appliance. It was a Merryweather Marquis pump escape of the very latest type, powered by a 125hp, six-cylinder AEC diesel engine, with a forward-control enclosed limousine type body. It was fitted with a centrally mounted major pump of 1,000gpm capacity which could supply eight deliveries and be operated from either side. A 100-gallon water tank supplied two top-mounted first-aid hose-reels and it carried a 50ft Merryweather wheeled escape.

It was soon to prove its worth. Building work on an extension to Woolworth's store in Strand Street, Douglas, was well advanced. At 10.15am on Wednesday, April 11 a tarpaulin between the store and the building works caught fire.

Mr Barlett, the manager, raised the

Fire at F W Woolworth in Strand Street, Douglas, on April 11, 1951. The wheeled escape from the Merryweather Marquis is in use on the front of the building while the appliance itself was in Howard Street.

alarm and evacuated customers from the store. He then led some of his staff in an ineffective attempt to fight the fire with hand extinguishers. He regrouped his staff on the stairs and formed a bucket chain but they had to retreat due to the heat of the fire, fanned by a strong south-westerly wind.

The fire brigade arrived within minutes of receiving the call, but the building was already well alight. Smoke was belching out of the top-floor windows and part of the roof collapsed before the second appliance arrived. The spread of fire was rapid; flames shot through the roof and threatened adjoining property. The first and second floors collapsed in a shower of burning debris.

The turntable ladder was in use as a water tower, directing a jet onto the flames. Firemen had to be withdrawn for a time from Strand Street as masonry was falling into the street. The front wall buckled and swayed as the internal floors and the rest of the roof fell away. Shortly afterwards the whole of the roof collapsed, leaving the front wall unsupported.

By this time the fire had jumped a natural gap and the rear of houses in Howard Street were vacated as flames licked roofs and window frames.

The brigade had the fire under control by noon, but it remained on duty through Wednesday night, breaking holes through the concrete pavement late in the evening to flood the basement and extinguish the last of the fire.

Shortly after this incident Mr Mayall arrived on the Island to take up his duties as Chief Fire Staff Officer to the Local Government Board. The various fire authorities were requested to prepare details of their establishment, as required under the Act which also made provision for mutual aid and pursuing powers. Mr Mayall prepared a reinforcement scheme for circulation to all participating fire authorities.

The scheme listed details of personnel and appliances to be made available to assist other fire authorities. Each scheduled appliance had to be complete with all ancillary gear and a minimum of 1,500ft of delivery hose. The reinforcing authority was required to send the appliance in charge of their seconded senior officer.

Schedule of reinforcing personnel and appliances

Authority	Personnel	Appliances/special apparatus
DOUGLAS	10	Major pump, 4 Proto sets, tender plus major trailer pump (or turntable ladder if needed)
RAMSEY	10	Tender plus major trailer pump and light trailer pump
CASTLETOWN	5	Tender plus major trailer pump
PEEL	5	Tender plus major trailer pump
LAXEY	5	Tender plus major trailer pump
MICHAEL	5	Tender plus light trailer pump
RUSHEN	5	Tender plus light trailer pump with 50ft escape

All appliances were required to carry foam compound and foam-making branch pipes.

After some minor difficulties agreement was eventually reached between the participating authorities, and the Fire Reinforcement Scheme, 1953, was submitted to Tynwald and approved on July 24.

Close liaison was maintained with RAF Jurby, and the Chief Fire Staff Officer could call on a trained body of men if required. Following the introduction of the reinforcement scheme the Commanding Officer at Jurby ordered an additional water tender to be made available by the station in case the need arose. Mr Mayall advised a programme of replacement, with strong emphasis on the need for pump water tenders.

The districts covered by the fire authorities were mainly rural, often without adequate water supplies. These appliances could be put into action as soon as they arrived at a fire. This advantage was readily grasped by the various brigades and the Local Government Board adopted the chief officer's recommendation as a matter of policy.

Although Douglas had opted out of the proposed all-Island scheme, discussions took place with the Douglas Fire Committee on the same subject and agreement was reached for the conversion of the existing Fordson tender. Work was put in hand for a 300-gallon tank to be installed within the bodywork and the light trailer pump to be fitted on the vehicle and permanently connected to a hose reel.

The Local Government Board lost no time in implementing the replacement programme and two new appliances were ordered for Peel and Castletown.

In February 1953 the Chief Fire Staff Officer and a fireman driver from Peel took delivery of the first new major pump water tender from Dennis Brothers at Guildford. The Dennis F8 was a self-propelled pump with a limousine-type body fitted with a 300-gallon water tank and a single first-aid hose-reel. The appliance carried delivery and suction hose and had locker space for all ancillary equipment. The Castletown appliance was delivered in June the same year.

An important move was made in 1953 by the Local Government Board towards the abolition of charges for brigade services. Negotiations took place between the Board and the Fire Officers' Committee representing the various insurance companies. Redemption money amounting to a sum of £32,500 was eventually agreed and sections 19 and 20 of the 1950 Act were repealed and amended by the Local Government (Fire Services) Act, 1954. This abolished payment to fire authorities and became effective from October 19, 1954.

A technical committee had been appointed in 1951 to look into the drafting of regulations under the Fire Escapes Act of 1950. These regulations were approved by the Local Government Board in November 1952 and passed by Tynwald the following month.

In March 1953 the Douglas Brigade was called to a fire at a five-storey boarding house in Palace Road, which once again underlined the need for such regulations. The alarm was raised shortly after 3am. When the brigade arrived, the fire had rapidly spread from the kitchen to the first and second floors. Damage to the main staircase had cut off the occupants of the upstairs rooms. They escaped through windows onto ladders put in place by neighbours.

The brigade found that the fire had a serious hold on the property, and was only contained with great difficulty. If a fire had occured in the height of the summer season the consequences could have been disastrous.

Ramsey Brigade had a call during the same month to a serious fire at Ballure Mount in which a man died. The property was occupied by a man of 70 living on his own. When the brigade arrived, the four-storey building was on fire from the basement to the third floor. It had obviously been burning for some time before the alarm was raised. The fire was brought under control more than 12 hours later, at about 9pm. An hour later the occupier's body was found in the debris, underlining the hazards of open fires and elderly people living alone.

The brigade was again called out, in October, this time to the Ramsey Gas Works, where the tar plant was found to be on fire. Faced with a very difficult and dangerous task, the brigade eventually extinguished the fire using new foam-making apparatus. The plant was severely damaged and a large gas main was cracked by the heat.

All the old wartime appliances which were surplus to requirements were taken into store by the Civil Defence Commission. A peacetime Auxiliary Fire Service was started, with an establishment of 75 men.

At the request of the Isle of Man Airports Board Mr Mayall arranged 72 training sessions during 1954 for the airport crash crews. By the start of 1955 the airport had a well-trained crew. Most of the Island's firemen had also been familiarised with the aircraft currently in use and the specialised fire-fighting equipment. The Island-reinforcing scheme was again put into operation in 1954 when fire broke out at King William's College.

At 9.45pm on May 11, smoke was seen coming from the roof of Dixon House. The college fire alarm was immediately sounded and the Castletown Brigade notified. Staff evacuated the dormitories on the first and second floors and the college fire brigade moved into action with a light pump connected to a hydrant in the quadrangle. They held the fire in check until the Castletown Brigade arrived shortly afterwards, reinforced by units from Rushen and Douglas. The fire was under control by 10.30pm but the brigade stayed until 5am the following morning.

This fire proved again the potential of an all-Island scheme and the need for a central fire control. This was to be a repeated request of successive Chief Fire Staff Officers, a request not granted until Douglas joined the all-Island scheme.

Continuing the programme of modernisation, a number of featherweight pumps were bought to replace the obsolete trailer pumps. The Rushen Fire Authority continued to provide a service covering the southern parishes and the two village districts of Port Erin and Port St Mary. The Authority still operated two stations, one in each village, with the escape carrier and trailer pump in Port Erin and the Austin towing vehicle and trailer pump in Port St Mary.

In 1951 the Authority embarked on the mammoth task of converting all the ball hydrants in its area. At the same time the Austin was converted to enable additional hose to be carried. Both stations were condemned as obsolete in 1955 and the Authority applied itself to providing a new central station.

The need for additional foam-making equipment had been worrying the Chief Fire Officer for some time. So he set about converting old trailer pump chassis into foam trailer units carrying 100 gallons of foam compound and two foam-making branch pipes. The first of these entered service in 1955; three were produced by the fire service's own staff.

Ramsey Brigade's appliances were now becoming obsolete and a further Dennis F8 was delivered to Ramsey in April 1955.

Later in the year the Austin towing vehicle kept by the Rushen Fire Authority at Port St Mary sub-station was sold to the Civil Defence Commission for £125. An Austin A30 van, complete with hose racks, was bought and stationed at Port Erin in the Falcon's Nest Yard, along with the escape carrier. The sub-station was closed down.

A site for the Rushen brigade's new fire station had been agreed with the Port Erin Commissioners: on their car-park adjoining Droghadfayle Road. It was completed in 1957 and opened on January 18 the following year by Mr A Moore of Port St Mary, who had been a member of the Rushen Fire Authority since its inception. The new station had a two-bay appliance room with lecture facilities.

During 1957 a joint police/fire radio communication scheme came into operation. Two sets were allocated to the fire service — one being installed in the Chief Fire Staff Officer's car and the other in the Ramsey first call appliance. With Douglas still outside the Island Fire Service, Ramsey was considered the main station. An additional set was acquired the following year and fitted to the Peel appliance.

In July 1958 a fire at Gretch Vane, Lonan, further emphasised the value of water tenders as means of getting water onto a fire quickly. Laxey brigade was called to a fire in the outbuildings of the farm. The appliance was the old Merryweather from Ramsey, now stationed at Laxey. Although it had a major pump and a portable ultra-lightweight pump, it did not carry water.

The nearest water supply was from a stream a quarter of a mile away. However, there was a water trough in the farmyard fed by a one-inch domestic supply. The ultra-lightweight pump was set up and the brigade was able to get two jets working immediately. The major pump was set up at the stream to relay water and supplement the supply to the trough. This kept the two jets in action, which was sufficient to bring the fire under control.

This was the first time that a portable lightweight pump had been used at a fire, and only the Rushen brigade remained without one.

Boy dies

The tragic death of a boy led to a warning from the fire service which would anticipate requirements which would later appear in by-laws.

Late in the afternoon of Saturday January 23, 1959, a neighbour ran to John Hyslop's home in Port St Mary and told him that smoke was pouring out of a house nearby. He called the brigade, and arrived at the house just before the appliance and the rest of the brigade.

They entered the building which was heavily smoke-logged, and searched for the seat of the fire. They found no obvious source and the house appeared to be empty. The house was vented and only then was smoke found to be issuing from a cupboard under the stairs.

Some smouldering paper and toys were easily extinguished. As they were clearing this rubbish the firemen were astonished to find a young boy in the cupboard, overcome by smoke.

Unsuccessful attempts were made at reviving him.

He had, it appeared, gone into the cupboard to look for toys by the light of a piece of burning paper. By some twist of fate the cupboard door had shut behind him.

The incident was a sad reminder of points which had been previously made in public by the fire service. Mr Mayall stressed again the importance of not leaving children on their own. He also cautioned against the use of door-latches which could only be operated from one side, anticipating requirements which would appear in bye-laws years later.

On September 16, 1959, the Rushen Fire Authority took delivery of a new Austin Gypsy self-propelled pump with four-wheel drive and a front-mounted 600gpm pump.

On the very day of delivery to the Rushen brigade it was called to a fire on Cronk ny Irree Laa which was threatening hundreds of acres of valuable grazing land.

The Dennis F28 wheeled escape allocated to Rushen Brigade being put through its paces during a demonstration on Port Erin promenade in 1962.

It was the only appliance that could get near to the fire ground which was two miles from the nearest water supply and several hundred feet above it. A road tanker was borrowed from Manx Petroleums and used to carry water to a point near the fire where it was relayed to the Gypsy, which was then able to provide pressure for two jets at the fire, in this way proving its worth beyond doubt.

The dry summer of 1959 caused all attendance records to be broken, with a year total of 382. The worst fire occurred in Archallagan Plantation; it destroyed 14 acres of trees and required a water relay of nearly a mile.

January 1, 1960, marked a great step forward for the fire service in the Island. The six fire authorities outside Douglas amalgamated into one, with a new committee of the Local Government Board, under the chairmanship of Lt J L Quine MHK, and representation from the old fire authority areas.

Meanwhile PC Kinrade had left Kirk Michael, being replaced by PC Moyer in 1951. He was approached by the Commissioners to take charge of the fire brigade; he accepted, having obtained the usual approvals. In October 1952, however, the Village Commissioners were notified by the Government Secretary that PC Moyer would no longer be able to continue as chief officer of the brigade due to a change of government policy. After considering the matter the Commissioners appointed Mr G E Creer as the new Chief Officer of their brigade.

The obsolete Merryweather at Laxey was replaced in June 1960 by a Dennis F28 pump water tender. The old appliance was relocated to Kirk Michael.

On March 23, 1961, a call was received shortly before midday by John Bell, Chief Officer of the Peel brigade, to a fire that followed an explosion in one of the diesel engines in Peel Power Station. On arrival he found the generating room heavily smoke-logged and immediately called for assistance from Douglas and Michael. The Douglas brigade was delayed at Glenvine by road-works and took 25 minutes to arrive, by which time its breathing apparatus was desperately needed.

The Chief Officer had been informed at the outset that the cranckcase of one of the large diesel engines had exploded, and two workmen were logged as missing. Entry was made and oil was found to be burning under the floor ducting, though all the other generating sets were still working.

The injured men, one of whom was severely burnt, were rescued and the engines shut down, though with some difficulty. This left a large part of the Island without electricity.

The fire was tackled by men in relays, using breathing apparatus. In the dense black smoke, the metal and concrete duct covers were lifted one at a time and the burning oil smothered with foam. The fire, eventually extinguished by 1pm, completely vindicated the provision of foam-generating equipment.

During the year a fifth foam trailer was commissioned at Castletown, leaving only Douglas and Laxey without. A further Dennis F28 with a wheeled escape was ordered for the Rushen brigade at a cost of £5,500, complete with a two-inch Alcon portable pump.

The previous year, Mr T A Kelly CBE MI, Fire Chief Officer of the Liverpool City Fire Brigade, had been commissioned to report on the all-Island scheme which had been under consideration since its preparation in 1956 by Mr Mayall. Now, in June 1961, his report was received. While it proved controversial in some respects, it did substantiate most of what had been said by Mr Mayall. The Douglas Brigade was singled out for special attention due to its unusal ranking system. This was reckoned to be out of line with current practice in the UK and as adopted by the rest of the Island. Attention was also focused on the age of some of its appliances — particularly the turntable ladder which dated from 1936.

The Douglas Corporation was understandably taken aback by the report and refuted some of the allegations. It defended the choice of chassis for the major pump, which had been quite properly made in relation to the fleet of AEC diesel buses operated and maintained by the Corporation. The Chief Officer also made the point that without a major pump of the size of the Merryweather Marquis, the Woolworth's fire of 1951 might have had a disastrous result. This appliance had taken water from one of nine special suction hydrants on the promenade and had rapidly distributed water to six branches: four at the fire and two at the properties in Howard Street.

However, the Corporation accepted criticisms of the age of the Dorman turntable ladder and the Albion/Merryweather, and asked Mr Courtie to report on their condition. Considering his recommendations, the council lost no time in ordering replacements. An AEC/Merryweather 100ft turntable ladder and a Dennis F28 water tender were delivered in 1962.

Mr Mayall resigned in September to become Chief Officer of Breconshire and Radnorshire Joint Fire Brigade, before he could see many of his ideas implemented. The Fire Services Committee made an approach to the Douglas Corporation and Mr Fred Courtie was appointed as acting Chief Fire Staff Officer until Mr Mayall's replacement was selected.

Mr Cyril Pearson became the new Chief Fire Staff Officer on September 1, 1962. At the request of the Fire Services Committee he prepared a report based on the two previous reports, and incorporated his own observations. Mr Pearson picked out one paragraph of the Kelly report as being vital to the issue..."It is not possible to obtain any reinforcements into the Island within a reasonable time and this is one of the problems which has to be appreciated and adequate fire cover provided within the Island itself..."

His recommendations endorsed much of what had been advocated by his predecessor. They included the provision of a new five-bay fire station at Douglas, with a central control and full-time staff as outlined in the Kelly report. He amplified Mayall's policy of giving each station a second appliance with a cross-country capability.

His priorities were the abolition of parochial boundaries, the establishment of a temporary all-Island fire control in Douglas

The Douglas brigade turns out to fight a fire on board the fishing vessel, Our Queen, in the town's harbour in February 1967. The major pump is an AEC Merryweather.

fire station, and the remote operation of fire warning devices at retained out-stations from that central control.

Kirk Michael station was the first to receive one of the new four-wheel drive appliances to Mr Pearson's design. It was based on a long-wheelbase Land Rover chassis with forward control, originally designed for military use. The contract for supply was won by a local firm, Shore Garages Ltd, with bodywork provided by Crosbie, Cain and Kennish of Douglas. The appliance was built in the company's premises and incorporated a 100-gallon water tank, pump, hose-reel, locker space and 30ft ladder. It was completed by September and entered service straight away, with a second going to Peel in February 1964.

In June 1963 a fire broke out at Ballaterson Manor, Ballaugh. The large house was gutted despite the efforts of the brigades in attendance, which were hampered by a poor water supply. Prior to the amalgamation the manor would have been on the limit of two fire authority areas, with all the attendant problems. On this occasion there was no confusion, the call being handled by central fire control and appliances being dispatched from Ramsey, Kirk Michael and Peel.

Five farm fires in the south of the Island the following year underlined the advantages of amalgamation, with multiple attendances at each fire by Castletown, Rushen, Peel and Douglas. This had been made possible by the terms of the Fire Authority Order, 1959, made by the Local Government Board and approved by all the fire authorities except Douglas, which nonetheless participated under its obligation to the reinforcement scheme.

Farm Fire

Tynwald had allocated £10,000 in 1958 for the improvement of water mains throughout the Island. Farmers had been encouraged to provide hydrants through an agricultural holdings grant-aid scheme. Despite these provisions there had been problems with the water supply at some farm fires. The situation in town and village areas was much better, but there were still improvements to be made. This was well illustrated by the problems encountered at one of the most difficult fires faced by the Rushen brigade.

In April 1964 it was called to a fire at Mallmore, a boarding house on Port St Mary promenade. Although the brigade was quickly on the scene, it found the roof already well alight. The men tackled the fire from the front of the building. However, the water main and hydrants were in a narrow lane to the rear, so hoses had to be laid round the block to the appliance. This meant a delay in getting water onto the fire. As soon as the pump was primed, the brigade was able to bring the fire under control. It was some time before it was eventually extinguished, however, due to pockets of fire in the roof space.

The implementation of the Fire Escapes Act and its regulations had been slow, but in 1961 Tynwald resolved to enforce Defect Orders under Section 7 of the Act with effect from March 21. The task facing the Island Fire Service was formidable, but the problem facing Douglas was worse. Douglas had by far the most

hotels and boarding houses. Although 639 buildings had been inspected since the introduction of the Act, 529 still had not been seen. Further, there were 1,500 premises which were still required to register. This work occupied the Chief Fire Officer of the Douglas Brigade virtually full-time. Following the Tynwald resolution, Douglas served defect notices on 186 owners of premises that needed outside escapes.

More escapes were needed than had been anticipated, so requests went back to Tynwald for more money to fulfil the grant provisions of the Act.

The Island lacked a completely unified service only because Douglas Corporation was unwilling to join the amalgamation scheme. This was due partly to civic pride, and to the fact that Douglas had the longest-serving brigade and was the only one with full-time personnel. The Corporation thought, perhaps justifiably, that any new system should evolve around its establishment. However, as the unified system was designed to cover the whole Island, it was quite proper that the new fire service should be administered by central government.

To bring matters to a head the Local Government Board presented a six-point report to Tynwald for approval, recommending that the Board should be the fire authority for the Douglas area. The recommendations were accepted and on June 16, 1964, Tynwald approved the Fire Authority Order, 1964.

The Fire Services Committee was reconstituted under the chairmanship of Mr H S Cain MHK, with Mr P Radcliffe MHK, Mr W E Fargher, Mr J J Quilliam and a representative from Douglas Corporation as members. From April 1, 1965 the Island at last had a unified fire service.

7. Unity at last

The all-Island fire service and the Summerland disaster

THE FIRST TASK facing the new Fire Services Committee was to reorganise the full-time staff. Within a very short time the new establishment emerged: Chief Fire Service Officer, Mr C Pearson; Asst Divisional Officer, Mr F Courtie; Station Officer, Mr H B Kenna; Sub Officers, Mr J Sloane, Mr R S Skinner, Mr J B Cowley, Leading Fireman Mr M Ventre, and three firemen to be appointed.

The policy of modernisation continued and Castletown's two-bay station opened in the early part of 1965 at Farrants Way. It replaced the obsolete premises in the Commissioners' Yard. Flashing lights and two-tone horns were fitted to appliances at about the same time as the rest of the UK.

The most important development took place on April 1, when Central Fire Control, manned on a 24-hour watch system, was at last established at Douglas station. At the same time, work started on a "999" emergency telephone call system.

In November there was a small fire in an electrical workshop at the rear of Express Radio in Athol Street. Douglas Brigade responded and the fire was quickly extinguished. During the attendance, however, a fireman collapsed and died. Ironically, this was Station Officer Kenna, whose father had been the only other Island fireman to die in service — some 27 years earlier.

The next new appliance to be delivered, in February 1967, was a Dennis F38 with a two-delivery rear-mounted pump and carrying a 50ft steel wheeled escape. It was commissioned and allocated to Ramsey. The following month the AFS — now administered by the Civil Defence Commission — took delivery of a Bedford Green Goddess Home Office pattern self-propelled pump designed following wartime AFS experience. The appliance carried a 1,000gpm pump and was the first of four to be delivered over the next year.

The integrated service was now responding to fires more quickly, and multi-brigade attendances were becoming a regular feature at major fires. During 1966 appliances from Ramsey, Laxey and Kirk Michael attended a serious fire at the Crossag farm near Ramsey. In January the following year another fire at Ballamoar, Lonan, required the attendance of appliances from Laxey, Ramsey and Douglas, with emergency lighting provided from an elderly Leyland emergency tender operated by the Civil Defence Commission.

This had been acquired by the Commission from the Glasgow City Fire Brigade, mainly for its capacity to provide light at any incident to which its personnel might have been called. The fire service was quick to realise its potential and it was again in use at a fire at the Maypole Supermarket in Strand Street, Douglas, in February 1967. Douglas station responded to the call, and reinforcements were immediately sent from Laxey and Peel.

The fire was difficult to contain, a task made worse by the presence of a false ceiling of polystyrene tiles. These tiles ignited, giving off dense acrid smoke, and fell in burning lumps on the firemen below. Breathing apparatus had to be used; despite this the fire was tackled directly from within. The turntable ladder was positioned at the rear of the building in Market Street, and the roof was perforated to assist with ventilation, until the fire was brought under control.

Implementation of the Fire Escapes Act still gave concern to the Chief Fire Staff Officer, following the earlier Tynwald resolution to enforce the defect notices. To remedy the situation, Fred Courtie became enforcing officer for the Act, taking up his appointment on April 5, 1966.

In his report for the year ending March 1967, Mr Pearson stressed the need for the urgent replacement of Douglas station with new premises, incorporating proper headquarters accommodation.

The John Street fire station was still the main one for Douglas, with insufficient space for more than one appliance. The Lord Street fire station was still the temporary wooden building dating from 1935, housing three appliances and incorporating the only maintenance bay. The headquarters staff and fire prevention department were housed in an old building in Christian Road, isolated from the rest of the brigade activity. The situation was obviously unsatisfactory.

Many sites were considered for the new Central Fire Station and a site on Peel Road was bought in 1974 for £14,000; building costs were £257,000. Meanwhile, in 1967, £12,000 had been earmarked for the building of a new fire station at Heathfield Drive for the Peel Brigade.

A Fire Liaison Panel was established the same year, following concern at the figures of wastage attributable to fire on the Island. This followed UK practice, when panels were formed at the instigation of the British Insurance Association to promote a better understanding of the consequences of fire and to stimulate better awareness of fire prevention.

The Tower Insurance Company took the initiative; with the drive of its manager, Mr G K Owen, a panel was formed from a broad cross-section of the business community.

During 1968 three new appliances were delivered. The first was a purpose-built emergency tender, fully equipped with cutting and handling gear, based on a long-wheelbase Land Rover chassis. The second was a Dennis F35 with a side-mounted pump with four deliveries and carrying a Merryweather 50ft wheeled escape. Both were stationed at Douglas, the Dennis replacing the Merryweather escape of 1951.

The third appliance was allocated to Rushen. It was the last of the four-wheel drive water tenders, based on the Land Rover, to have been built locally. It was slightly different from the others, incorporating modifications borne out of operational experience.

The last major incident attended by the old pump escape was a fire at Parkfield, Douglas, in June 1968. The fire started in a harness room at the rear of the house and spread to a bedroom above. There was a full turnout of the Douglas brigade; the men managed to confine the fire to the rear of the house, but not before considerable damage had been done.

A Dennis F46A water tender with a 500 gpm pump and two deliveries, carrying 400 gallons of water, was delivered in April 1971. Stationed at Douglas, it become the first-call appliance, replacing the F28 of 1962 which was transferred to Castletown as part of the continuing policy of updating the Island service.

One of the Green Goddess Bedford appliances, allocated to the Civil Defence Commission for use by the AFS, was transferred to the regular fire service, painted red and also stationed at Castletown. The station was then equipped with one 500 gpm and one 1,000 gpm pump, considered essential in view of its proximity to Ronaldsway Airport. In the event of an emergency at the airport, Castletown would be the nearest reinforcing brigade.

The fire station at Ramsey, beneath the Town Hall, had been unsatisfactory for years. It housed two appliances — one behind the other — which caused frequent operational difficulties. When the Town Commissioners announced in 1970 that they intended to demolish the Town Hall, the Fire Service Committee had to look for an alternative site. Tynwald approved £25,000 for the provision of a new station with a three-bay appliance room, adjoining lecture room, recreational facilities, practice ground and tower.

Summerland

July 1971 saw the opening of the Summerland leisure complex. It was a pioneering development providing a wide variety of entertainment. The building was wonderful in concept: a huge area covered by a transparent cladding of acrylic material. It had been built by the Douglas Corporation and let to Trust House Forte Leisure Ltd.

The northern part of the building incorporated a multi-level entertainment area, including a marquee show bar, leisure deck and a ground-floor amusement arcade. Families could spend a carefree day here, in the light and airy atmosphere, enjoying the amenities. The leisure area was connected to a solarium by open flying staircases. Many seaside resorts on the UK mainland were planning similar complexes.

Then, on then evening of August 2, 1973, some boys accidentally set fire to a dismantled kiosk on an outside terrace, and this small fire spread to the main building. The aftermath was to bring dramatic changes to the legislation governing fire safety on the Island, and leave its mark on the whole of the British Isles. It was the worst peace-time disaster involving fire since 1929.

The fire was discovered at 7.40pm on the Mini Golf terrace outside the main building. The alarm was raised at staff level within Summerland and they set about tackling the blaze with hand extinguishers and a hose reel. Their efforts had little effect.

At 8.01pm the Central Fire Control received a telephone call from Duggans Radio Cabs, via 999, that Summerland was on fire. This was followed by others in quick succession, one via Douglas Harbour Radio from a ship anchored in Douglas Bay.

Appliances were dispatched at 8.02pm with sub-officer Quayle as the senior officer in the first-call appliance. By 8.08pm he was on the Promenade and could see that the fire was serious. He called by radio for pumps and the turntable ladder.

The first message from Summerland was not received until the appliances were on their way. The automatic alarm — a two-stage device with a direct link to Douglas Fire Service Station — was not activated until 8.05pm.

The building had eight levels within the external cladding. Officer Quayle cleared the downstairs and upper downstairs levels but was unable to gain access to the main solarium floor level due to the heat and burning debris falling from the roof.

At this time there was extensive fire on all three terraces above the amusement arcade where the fire had entered the building. The transparent cladding had nearly all been enveloped in a rapid surface spread of fire, which gave off asphyxiating and explosive vapours and allowed burning molten plastic to fall on the exposed stairways and floors.

An all-stations alert was made at 8.10pm; 15 minutes later

they were all mobile. Altogether 14 appliances attended, although by 3am the following day most had returned to their stations.

When the Chief Fire Staff Officer arrived at the fire it was immediately apparent to him that nothing could be done to save the Summerland building. Instead he concentrated efforts on stopping the fire at the southern boundary; this realistic approach meant that the nearby Aquadome building was unscathed.

Water pressure for fire-fighting purposes was barely adequate, despite the presence of six fire hydrants in the vicinity of the building. Following urgent calls from the fire service, engineers from the water authority were able to improve the situation. By 9.10pm the fire was under control. During the following day, the out-stations were recalled to carry out damping-down operations and provide relief for the Douglas Brigade.

However, firemen stayed at Summerland for three more days. On the Friday after the fire, out-of-town brigades were still in attendance, providing relief for the Douglas men who had been on duty through the night.

On Saturday 4, Douglas brigade dealt with a number of small outbreaks. Out-of-town brigades were again in attendance on the Sunday until about 6pm, damping down and clearing up.

When the fire broke out there were 3,000 people in Summerland. Fifty of them died trying to escape. Fire damage to the building approached £1.5m.

On September 3, the Lieutenant Governor of the Island appointed a Commission of Inquiry, under the chairmanship of the Hon Mr Justice Cantley OBE, to inquire into and report on the circumstances of the fire. The enquiry lasted until February 1974, and the report was published in May.

Three main reasons were found for the large number of deaths: the very rapid development of the fire, the inadequate means of escape, and the evacuation of the building being delayed, unorganised and difficult. Many family members had tried to find one another; this also hindered the evacuation, with tragic consequences.

The absense of any fire stops either horizontal or vertical between the outer cladding and the inner lining resulting in the

Fire gutted the Douglas Holiday Centre in the summer of 1972, the night after Duke Ellington and his band had appeared. The Douglas AEC Merryweather 100ft turntable ladder is shown fighting the blaze at the rear of the stage area.

rapid spread of the fire, which in turn set fire to the inner fibreboard linings and the interior finishings. The multi-storey part of the building was very quickly engulfed in fire.

There were 20 "break-glass" fire alarm points and seven staff points, all directly connected to the Douglas fire station and to an internal two-stage alarm system. The Commission found that 25 minutes elapsed before any alarm was actuated and even then no alarm sounded within Summerland itself.

It also found shortcomings in the escape routes from the building. The worst instance was a supposedly protected staircase into which a permanent opening had been made. This allowed smoke to penetrate the area and this, coupled with the failure of the emergency lighting system and the fact that the emergency doors at the bottom of the stairway were bolted, resulted in the death of 12 people.

The Commission concluded with 34 recommendations, many of which had far-reaching consequences. It had much to say about the use of certain types of building materials, particularly plastics. The outcome was that the British Standards Institute set about revising certain codes of practice and technical data.

It was recommended that any fire alarm system installed in a public place should always fail to an alarm state and not be capable of being switched off by unauthorised persons.

It recommended that architectural training should include a much extended study of fire protection and fire precautions. This resulted in the Royal Institute of British Architects reviewing its professional code of conduct and, as an interim measure, publishing a booklet the following July entitled *Fire and the Architect*.

Turning to the Island, the Commission urged the immediate revision of theatre regulations and building bye-laws. These two single recommendations drastically changed the whole approach to fire safety, involving the fire service to a much greater extent and paving the way for an even more unified service.

The United Kingdom Fire Precautions Act, 1971, did not apply to the Isle of Man, but its contents had been under consideration even before the Summerland fire. It was obvious that something had to be done quickly. Urgent legislation was introduced in the form of the Local Government (Fire Services

Amendment) Act 1974 which became effective from October. It gave the Fire Services Committee powers to charge for special services, and to enter, inspect and control fire exits.

In October 1975 these powers were incorporated in greater detail in the Fire Precautions Act, 1975. The Fire Escapes Act, 1950, was repealed and new requirements incorporated in the revised legislation. Fire certificates became compulsory for certain premises.

The Act covered public buildings, hotels, boarding houses and certain types of residential premises, requiring adequate means of escape and specifying other fire precautions. The Local Government Board made a number of enforcing orders; suddenly the full implications of the new Act became apparent.

The Board had also set about revising its building bye-laws, following the recommendation of the Commission, and in April 1976 they took effect. One section of the new bye-law document related entirely to structural fire precautions and means of escape. There was particular emphasis on compartmentalising and the provision of fire stops: both were lessons learned from the Summerland fire.

Fire prevention

Mr Pearson's retirement as Chief Fire Staff Officer saw his replacement by Mr J Hinnigan, Member of the Institute of Fire Engineers, on September 1, 1974. Mr Hinnigan had been involved in the discussions with the committee which had drafted the new bye-laws, and was thus under no illusions about the workload that would fall on the fire service. A fire prevention department was set up with four station officers and one acting station officer working under the direction of Assistant Divisional Officer Whiteford, the senior Fire Prevention Officer.

In May 1975 the fire service took delivery of an SS220 Simon Snorkel hydraulic platform, based on a 6.5-litre ERF chassis. The platform operated to a height of 22 metres (72ft); it could be controlled from the ground or from the platform itself, which carried a monitor with built-in delivery fixed to the booms. The duplicate controls fitted to the base of the platform had an override capability, allowing the ground operator to intervene in case of emergency. The appliance also carried a lightweight portable Godiva pump.

The platform was allocated to Douglas; it could have been housed in John Street station, though its length would have made access difficult. It was too big for the Lord Street station so, as a temporary measure, it was garaged at the Douglas Gas Works Industrial Estate until the completion of the Central Fire Station. It was stationed at John Street on occasions when the turntable ladder was off the run, and it made several visits to Ramsey fire station.

The service took delivery, also in May, of a water tender fitted with a 500gpm pump and similarly based on an ERF chassis. It carried 400 gallons of water and was fitted with standard aluminium ladders. The appliance was allocated to Peel, replacing the Dennis F8 of 1953. In the early part of 1980 it was converted to take the steel-wheeled escape from the Dennis F35 pump escape at Douglas, which then became the spare appliance.

In the early part of 1977 the Isle of Man Fire Service took possession of the new Peel Road Central Fire Station and Headquarters, which are still in use today. The formal opening took place on June 30.

The station was basically the five-bay station that had been recommended by Mr Mayall some 20 years earlier. The appliance room is served by four of the five doors and, because of its unusual layout, can house seven appliances. The fifth bay is devoted to the service facilities provided by the full-time transport officer and civilian mechanic.

To the rear of the appliance room are full stores facilities for all the stations on the Island, along with service and re-charging facilities for breathing apparatus. The first floor houses the administration staff, with offices for the chief and deputy officers, together with lecture, recreation and canteen facilities. The rest of the ground floor provides accommodation for the Fire Prevention Department, radio equipment and the control room which is the nerve centre of the Island Fire Service.

The control room is continually manned and all 999 calls are directed to it. The control panel affords the duty firemen full radio contact with all appliances and also to switchboard telephone and recording facilities. An automatic call system activates personal pocket radio alerters and simultaneously sets off the respective station sirens. At out-of-town stations, the first retained fireman to arrive answers the telephone; this cancels the siren and he then receives notification of the location of the fire from central control.

In the daytime the duty crew can man the first appliance and leave the station within seconds of the call being received; an internal broadcast system to all parts of the station notifies the location and nature of the fire. The off-duty crew and retained men are alerted in the normal way, arriving at the station within minutes to man additional appliances as required. Outside the station there is a large training ground and practice tower with full circulation round the station.

Shortly after the Fire Services Committee took possession of the new headquarters, a further ERF (similar to the Peel appliance) was delivered and stationed at Castletown. It became the first-call machine and released the other F8 which dated from 1953. This older machine was taken into the central fire station and converted into a foam-carrying hose layer. It carried 300 gallons of foam compound and 1,500ft of hose — ready coupled and capable of being laid at 10mph.

Production of beer at Okell's Glen Falcon Brewery, Douglas, was interrupted following a fire which broke out near the lift-motor room in the roof space on Thursday, October 27, 1977. It completely destroyed part of the roof and the five-storey building was water-damaged. However firemen, under the direction of Station Officer Whiteford, were able to place salvage sheets over the vats and thus prevent damage to their contents.

Fire appliances from Douglas, Laxey and Peel were in attendance with 30 firemen. The fire was under control in half an hour but the brigade stayed all afternoon to clear up and secure the building, some 25,000 gallons of water having been used in extinguishing the fire, most of it being discharged through the turntable ladder monitor.

A month later another fire broke out at the same brewery, but this time in the bottling store. The fire was deep-seated in plastic crates, which generated great heat and gave off acrid smoke. The fire was tackled from within and contained, the firemen using breathing apparatus and working in relays. Priority was given to venting the store and the turntable ladder was again used to give additional cover from above while venting was taking place.

Six appliances attended initially under Station Officer Cain, later joined by the Chief Fire Staff Officer, in view of the suspicious nature of the fire following so close after the earlier one. The fire was, in fact, treated by the police as suspected arson.

Continuing its programme of modernisation, the fire service took delivery of a new water tender in May 1978. This was a Dennis R61 carrying 400 gallons of water and fitted with a 500 gpm pump. It was allocated to Kirk Michael, reflecting the area's population growth, and allowing the Land Rover to be transferred to Ramsey.

As a temporary measure the new appliance was housed together with the Austin Gypsy in the old station, a relic of the wartime AFS measures, until the new station was completed in the former railway goods shed off Station Road. A second R61 was delivered in February 1979 and allocated to Ramsey, replacing the Dennis F8 dating from 1955.

All stations except Laxey now had two appliances, at least one of which was a major pumping unit. The brigade had full radio communication with all appliances operating through central control. All personnel were equipped with personal radio alerters; they could justifiably be described as an efficient brigade functioning as a single unit. The old boundaries had disappeared; from now on the nearest appliance to the fire was turned out, with automatic reinforcement from adjoining stations.

Lodging house fire

The system was put to the test on March 17, 1979, at a major fire in a Douglas lodging house. The fire was almost certainly first noticed by two policemen on motor patrol in the lower part of the town. Sgt McHarrie and PC Corlett saw smoke at about 3.15am and set about investigating its source. They soon traced it to 19 Belmont Terrace which was found to be on fire with smoke and flames belching from the front door. Entry was impossible and they immediately radioed for fire brigade and police assistance.

People in the house were wakened by the noise of the fire and one of the lodgers screaming. The noise woke a next-door neighbour, Mr Corris; he was unsure what was happening until he saw black smoke coming into his room through the party wall.

The radio alerters were operated and within five minutes the first appliance had left the station, in the charge of Leading Fireman Counsel. Two minutes later the water tender, in the charge of Sub-officer Christian, had been despatched. The first appliance arrived at the fire ground at 3.32am, at the same time as the duty officer, Assistant Divisional Officer Cain. Meanwhile, some of the house's 11 occupants had made use of the fire escape at the rear, although access to it was severely hampered by dense black smoke and heat.

Officer Cain was informed by the police that six people were unaccounted for. Three jets were immediately brought into use, but entry was impossible from the front due to intense heat and flame. At 3.39am a message, "make pumps five", was sent, and the duty watch-keeper activated Peel, Castletown and Laxey alerters. The turntable ladder was pitched at the front of the building and Fireman Cunningham manned the monitor to direct water on the fire at second floor level.

Deputy Chief Officer Hopkin took charge at the front of the building, with Divisional Officer Ventre taking charge of a party to prevent spread of fire to the adjacent properties.

With men from Douglas and Laxey, Officer Cain gained entry at the rear and rescued the owner and his wife; they were taken to hospital where the woman was found to be dead through suffocation.

The Chief Fire Officer arrived shortly before 4am and took overall control. With Peel and Castletown in attendance, seven jets were in use but little impression was being made on the fire. At 4.20am the chief sent the message "make pumps eight" and Ramsey and Kirk Michael were alerted. At 5.50am the fire, which had also broken into number 18, was surrounded; by 6.30am it was effectively out. Three bodies were found in the debris.

The inquest found, after studying forensic evidence, that the fire had been started by a carelessly-dropped cigarette which had set fire to soft furnishings. The foam-filled padding had created heat and dense smoke. The heat had caused the gas cylinder in a room heater to blow a relief valve, thus avoiding a potentially catastrophic explosion. But the free flow of gas instantly ignited and fuelled the fire, causing excessive heat at the seat of the fire.

Despite the deaths, the response to the fire clearly illustrated the efficiency of the Island Fire Service. As with all serious fires, the service was quick to analyse its performance and learn from it. One of the outcomes was the drawing up of clear and concise control room procedures with predetermined attendances of appliances for classes and zones of premises.

In June a new Ford A-Series emergency tender was delivered and stationed at Douglas. The appliance was built by Cheshire Fire Engineering and was complete with air lifting bags, full electric and air-operated cutting gear and jacking. It also carried a large cluster floodlight mounted on an extending telescopic mast, powered by a built-in $2^1/_2$ Kw electric generator. This generator also provided power for the tools and portable lighting. Additional equipment included a portable 2Kw generator set, lighting set and a small three-section ladder.

It quickly proved its worth in dealing with the increasing number of traffic accidents, and was a revolutionary tool at night-time fires. It was not surprising that the service was quick to incorporate a number of its features in one of the Leyland Sherpa vans, stationed at Ramsey, creating another emergency tender fitted with a stalk light and cutting gear.

The Fire Service took delivery in May 1980 of a Dennis RS 61 water tender to replace the pump escape at Douglas which then became the reserve appliance. The new vehicle was fitted with a 1,000gpm pump with four deliveries and carried 400 gallons of water. Its most unusual feature, as far as the Island was concerned, was that it carried a 45ft Angus 464 extending ladder instead of a wheeled escape.

The appliance filled the need for a large-capacity pump to power the trailer-mounted Jetmaster Foam Monitor. This was an extremely important consideration in view of the large quantities of liquid petroleum gas and fuel oils stored in the vicinity of Douglas harbour. Operational orders were drawn up and code-named Operation Oil Fire, and exercises were mounted.

Despite the presence of large quantities of water, tidal conditions often made it impossible to take suction from the sea to feed the drencher installations. The Local Government Board provided a static water tank with a capacity of 250,000 gallons in the Harbour Board yard for fire-fighting purposes.

The two new appliances attended their first major fire at about 11pm on Friday, December 5, 1980 at the Peveril Hotel, Douglas — one of the Island's largest and oldest hotels.

The fire broke out in the east wing; fanned by a stiff breeze it soon engulfed the top floors. The hotel occupied almost two sides of a square and, with restricted access at the rear and a petrol station abutting it, this proved to be a difficult fire to attack.

It was fought from above by monitors on the turntable ladder situated on the promenade, and the hydraulic platform in Peveril Square. Firemen were also able to use hoses on the rear of the building and managed to confine the fire to the east wing. Wearing breathing apparatus, they also tackled the fire from within the building.

Altogether 11 fire appliances attended; at one time eight pumps were in use. Fifty firemen fought the fire and brought it under control by 3am on Saturday. Twenty sets of breathing apparatus were used. Having broken through the roof, the fire completely destroyed the upper floors of the east wing. The rest of the building was affected by water and smoke, with damage being caused to curtains and decorations. The fire service was in attendance on Saturday and Sunday, damping down and making the building safe.

There is no doubt that the fire service has undergone more changes in the years since 1975 than at any other time in its history. The amount of legislation passed by Tynwald, and Orders made by the Local Government Board, bear witness to this. The emphasis is on safety to the public in places of entertainment, hotels and boarding houses.

The effects of the Fire Precautions (Hotel and Boarding Houses) Order, 1976, and the Housing (Flats) Regulations, 1979, made under the Housing (Miscellaneous Provisions) Act are perhaps

Fire broke out at the Peveril Hotel, Douglas, on December 5, 1980, and it took 50 firemen, 11 appliances and eight pumps, working through the night, to bring it under control.

the most noticeable to the public. Premises are required to be registered; adequate means of escape, and separate access to individual flats, have to be provided. Emergency lighting, smoke-detecting equipment and automatic fire alarms must be fitted. Compartmentalising is also required, with the provision of smoke doors, ventilated lobbies and self-closing doors within flats and similar accommodation.

Hidden in this mass of legislation was one extremely important Act, which set out to establish a Civil Aid Services Planning Committee to co-operate in case of a major emergency on the Island. Included in its terms of reference was a brief to make advance planning for the control, co-ordination and administration of all emergency services. This was incorporated in the Civil Aid Services (Planning) Act, 1976.

On April 24, 1981, an incident occurred which had not been anticipated in any emergency planning procedures. A family were driving, in severe snow conditions, over the Snaefell mountain road from Douglas to Ramsey. They had ignored the "Road Closed" signs erected earlier in the day. The car became stuck in a drift near the Bungalow at about 3pm. The driver found his way

73

with difficulty to the Crag ny Baa Hotel and raised the alarm, being concerned for the safety of the car's occupants who included an elderly person and a young child.

The police and highway authority were notified, and snow-ploughs were sent from Douglas, Ramsey and Sulby. They made little progress, however, in what were now blizzard conditions.

It became known that two telephone engineers who had been working on the mountain road were also stranded nearby. Contact was made by police who had travelled part-way by the Snaefell Mountain Railway and then walked the rest of the way along the railway track.

By 6.10pm it was realised that very little progress was being made by the snowploughs; indeed one had become firmly stuck. The fire service offered two of its four-wheel drive appliances to assist the Highway Board in its attempt to reach the stranded people by way of Tholt y Will.

A large tracked excavator from a nearby construction site was eventually used, and contact with the stranded people made shortly after 11pm. They were brought part of the way down by the excavator and then transferred to the fire service vehicles for the rest of the trip.

The upshot of this has been the setting up of a mountain rescue team made up from police and fire service personnel, using existing equipment and vehicles.

Earlier in the year the Local Government (Fire Services) Act, 1981, was passed; it abolished the fire service rate and the fire fund with effect from May 1980. The service became completely funded from central government from that date. At about the same time a new Control Room Procedure was introduced into the brigade operational orders. It dealt with numerous control room procedures in respect of the Multitone Alerter radio system and the Automatic Fire Alarm Panel. Its most important features were to revise the specified predetermined first attendance for various classes of high-risk property. Public buildings and residential property required three major pumps, the emergency tender and turntable ladder. In the Douglas area this required an automatic turnout of appliances from Laxey, Peel or Castletown, depending on the exact location of the fire.

The efficient brigade radio scheme operates on both VHF and UHF frequencies. This means that the officer in charge of a fire ground can mobilise full brigade resources through the central control room within seconds of arrival.

The predetermined attendance orders work on the principle that each fire is a major incident. The senior officer can assess the situation on arrival and can, if necessary, recall any appliance not required. The advantage of this system is that valuable minutes are saved on call-out and attendance time if a fire turns out to be major.

A further four-wheel drive appliance, based by Pilcher-Green on the Land Rover chassis, entered service in June 1981. Fitted with an integral rear-mounted pump it carried a single hose reel, 100 gallons of water and a small extension ladder. It was attached to Kirk Michael station, allowing the Austin Gypsy to be transferred to Laxey, thus giving the station a second appliance for the first time.

With only Douglas and Castletown still without a four-wheel drive appliance, the opportunity was taken at the same time to acquire two Austin Gypsy vehicles from the Civil Defence Commission which were surplus to requirements. Altered and adapted for fire service use in the brigade workshops, they entered service towards the end of 1981 at Castletown and at Douglas early in 1982, completing the policy introduced by Mr Mayall in 1959.

In December a new Dennis DS Series pump water tender entered service, with a 500gpm pump and carrying 400 gallons of water. It was allocated to Laxey and replaced the Dennis F28 which was transferred to the Civil Defence Commission for AFS use.

Just as the Isle of Man Fire Service had reached the pinnacle of its development it found itself at yet another crossroads. The Home Affairs Board Bill, 1981, was presented to the House of Keys in June, 1981, and the future of the fire service was very much tied up in the Bill. Its object was to establish one single Board of Tynwald to take over certain functions relating to the fire service. The Bill was signed at a sitting of Tynwald on October 13, 1981. Following a General Election held in November, a new Home Affairs Board was established.

8. Modern times

The service through the 1980s; formation of the Isle of Man Fire & Rescue Service

THE YEAR 1982 was a hectic one for the service; a number of major fires occurred from which, as always, lessons were learned. A 999 call at 6.12pm on March 6 reported a fire in a building in Bucks Road, Douglas, occupied by Neil Kelly's motorcycle showroom.

The first appliance arrived six minutes later and reported "make pumps four". Peel and Laxey stations were alerted to provide additional support. The fire started in the workshop at the rear of the showroom, when a spark ignited the gas from batteries that were being recharged. It spread quickly to the showroom, engulfing motorcycles and tyres. The proprietor re-entered the building wearing a nylon shop coat and attempted to extinguish the flames himself and remove some of the stock. He was overcome and detained in hospital for a week suffering from burns and the effects of smoke inhalation. The fire was intense; at its peak it required four jets and breathing apparatus to be used.

ADO Whitefield sent the stop call at 6.41pm; by 9.35pm fire fighting had finished and adjoining properties had been made secure. Nothing was left of the showroom, and the motorcycles were reduced to piles of molten metal. It highlighted the care that must be taken when charging batteries, and emphasised the golden rule of fire safety: never re-enter a building after discovering fire.

An incident six days later involved the IoM Steam Packet Company's vessel, *NF Jaguar*; on which a container had fallen onto a trailer of propane cylinders. On arrival the fire officer in charge found nitram fertilizer in the container: a potentially disastrous cocktail because adjacent cargo included a heated tanker of bitumen.

It took two hours to retrieve the container and check the propane cylinders, during which time Douglas brigade had two jets and two ground monitors in place as a precaution. It illustrated the need to take care when loading vessels, having regard to the interaction between differing cargoes, especially those that could explode. These lessons were learned by both the shipping company and the fire service.

In April, Laxey Glen Gardens cafe and associated buildings were gutted by fire in the middle of the night, requiring attendance from Laxey and Douglas brigades. At the height of the blaze, five jets were in use and it was four hours before the fire service was stood down.

One of the most unusual 999 calls came from the Ramsey Coastguard at 9.27am on Friday, August 6, reporting a fire at Snaefell Summit Hotel. Laxey and Ramsey Brigades were alerted. There is no road to the summit — 621 metres (2,037ft) above sea level — so the Laxey brigade got to the top the same way that thousands of tourists do every year: an electric tramcar from the Snaefell Mountain Railway was requisitioned and the firemen made off for the summit with a wagon carrying 300 gallons of water. At 10.12am, Station Officer Boyd reported to Douglas Fire Control that the Summit Hotel was burnt out.

The fire had probably burned all night after the building had been vacated. Although only about three miles in a direct line from the Laxey fire station, it had taken the crew 45 minutes to reach the summit.

It was to Laxey later in the year that the chairman of the Home Affairs Board came, to open the new two-bay fire station. It was on a new site in Mines Road, not far from the old wartime station, completing the Island-wide programme of modernisation begun in 1965 with the new Castletown station. Port Erin station had been modernised earlier while still under the Rushen Fire Authority.

As part of the continuing process of modernisation, another Dennis DS appliance was purchased in 1983 at a cost of £42,500, and allocated to Port Erin. These short wheelbase appliances proved invaluable in both rural and urban areas, their small turning circle allowing them access to areas where larger appliances could not venture.

Because of the extra equipment being carried on a chassis limited to an 8.5 tons gross vehicle weight, the water carried when the wheeled escape was fitted was limited to 200 gallons. Otherwise the vehicle carried all the usual equipment of a DS, including a 500gpm pump with two deliveries and two standard first-aid hose reels.

A further DS appliance was delivered the following year and allocated to Castletown, replacing the F28 which had originally belonged to the Douglas Brigade. This older appliance was retained, becoming the foam tender/hose layer and replacing the older Dennis F8 at Douglas.

The Fire Services Act, 1984, repealed the Local Government Fire Services Acts and consolidated the provisions, vesting authority in the Home Affairs Board. One outcome of the Act was the redesignation of the Chief Officer of the brigade as the Chief Fire Officer and it clarified that no charge should be made by the brigade for fire-fighting purposes.

Air-sea rescue

The years of training with helicopters from RAF Valley in Anglesey for incidents at sea were put to good use, in 1985, though not for fire-fighting purposes. The fire service received a call from Noble's Hospital just before noon on April 17, and was instructed to prepare the landing site at King George V Park for a helicopter, which was to land shortly with an injured seaman on board. This was followed by a message from Ramsey Coastguard that fire brigade personnel might be needed to release a man trapped in a winch on the fishing vessel *Wendy Anne*. The brigade mobilised to await further instructions and at 12.45pm, ADO Cain, Sub-officer Simpson and leading fireman Warriner were lifted to the fishing vessel. A doctor was already on board.

Work proceeded on cutting cables and other gear, while the vessel made for Douglas. It berthed at 1.15pm at the Victoria Pier, where the emergency tender was used to power hydraulic spreaders to remove the winch drum. Fifteen minutes later the man was released, having sustained severe injuries. He was transferred to Noble's Hospital for emergency surgery and the winchman was returned by fire personnel to the helicopter at the landing site.

Another fire in November 1985 presented difficult problems for the fire service and could have changed the face of Laxey. A 999 call was received at control in Douglas from Mr Cowin at 2.40am, reporting a fire near the famous Laxey Wheel. Four minutes later Station Officer Boyde acknowledged the call from Laxey fire station; having seen the glow in the sky he requested requested "pumps three"; an additional pump was despatched from Douglas before anyone had reached the fire.

The Wheel Café, a timber-framed building, was totally engulfed in the fire. Radiated heat was threatening the world's largest water wheel, built to serve the lead and silver mines of Laxey. At 6.10am, a request was made for an additional pump appliance to protect the wheel, which was largely built of timber. Several minutes later the building collapsed and radiated heat ignited a car parked nearby.

The fire remained seated in the basement of the brick-built building. It was almost four hours before the fire service could pack up and return to the station. At the height of the blaze there were four jets and one ground monitor in use. Although the pretty café, resembling a Swiss chalet, was lost, the fire service was able to contain the fire. The Laxey Wheel, threatened by the flames, was saved.

A fire in Lindon Grove in Douglas was a reminder to the Chief Fire Officer about the problems that could still be encountered in old properties, where there are common roof spaces above individual properties. The incident was also a timely reminder for firemen to take care over the spread of fire. This same point was further illustrated in March 1987, at Bretney Estate in Jurby, this time involving modern houses built to current bye-law standards. The area is some distance, in Isle of Man terms, from the nearest fire station and nearly equidistant from Ramsey and Kirk Michael.

A 999 call reported a fire in a two-storey house on the estate at 10.10pm. Ramsey and Kirk Michael brigades were alerted and the first Ramsey appliance arrived 12 minutes later. They quickly got to work with one jet and firemen wearing breathing apparatus; both hose reels were in use. The occupant had been overcome by smoke but neighbours had rescued her before the brigade arrived. The ground floor of the house was well alight on arrival; even with Kirk Michael R61 in attendance, and three jets in use, the fire could not be contained.

ADO Cain took charge on arrival and requested "pumps four". Laxey was alerted and a Douglas appliance sent to Ramsey to provide cover, but it was diverted when the request was increased to "pumps five" and the hydraulic platform, as three houses were now involved in the fire. Shortly after 11pm, the roof of number 15, where the blaze had started, partially collapsed, and flames spread to the roof of the second house. The fire was eventually stopped in the roof of the third house, having been surrounded by five jets and three hose reels, with appliances from Ramsey, Kirk Michael, Douglas, Laxey and Peel in attendance.

A Kirk Michael fireman received an injury to his hand that required hospital treatment, and the occupant of the house where the fire started was admitted to Ramsey Cottage Hospital suffering from shock and smoke inhalation. The Salvation Army gave help to those who had been evacuated.

The stop call came from ADO Cain just before midnight, almost two hours after the first call, though the brigade was actually in attendance for nine hours. Three houses out of a terrace of six had been involved, and the fire had spread at roof level. There was smoke damage to the remaining properties due to percolation through the roof void.

The fire service, like many other government departments, had been swept up in reorganisation with the introduction of a system of ministerial government on the Island. From April 1, 1986, the fire service found itself part of the Department of Home Affairs which was also responsible for the police. The Hon E G Lowey MLC was appointed Minister for the Department and he appointed Mr A C Duggan MHK as Chairman of the Fire Services Committee, with delegated powers. The other member of the committee was Councillor Fred Waterson. Their first task was to review the appliance replacement programme and then examine the full-time manning levels of the brigade.

In 1987 the service acquired the first of a new breed of all-terrain appliances: a Fulton & Wylie appliance on a Mercedes 1300L Unimog chassis. A far cry from the early 4 x 4 vehicles, it carried 6,300 gallons of water, a front-mounted twin delivery pump, four sets of breathing apparatus and a 10.5 metre Angus/Sarol ladder in addition to the usual small tools and ancillary items. After full evaluation and acceptance trials at brigade headquarters, the appliance was allocated to Laxey.

There were a number of fires in the lower part of Peel later the same year, culminating in a fire on October 21 at 7 Charles Street. This intense fire occurred after midnight; access was difficult due to cars parked in the narrow streets nearby. Attending the blaze were two appliances from Peel and one from Douglas. Firemen wearing breathing apparatus rescued three people, two of whom were removed to hospital after receiving medical treatment at the scene. Questions were asked subsequently regarding access for emergency vehicles, and the need to enforce parking restrictions.

Gas leaks at various times during the previous decade eventually led to additional legislation. The Fire Services (Amendment) Act, 1990, gave the power to evacuate property, in the event of an emergency, to any constable or member of the fire brigade of leading fireman rank or above. This piece of legislation is unique in the British Isles and follows on from the lessons learnt at two incidents.

The first occurred on September 21, 1983, when men employed by the Douglas Gas Light Company were working on a main at the South Quay near to the entrance to the gasworks. The work involved the use of a grinding wheel; sparks ignited gas in a pipe, causing an explosion in the pump house that damaged a large spade valve.

Appliances from Douglas, Castletown, Peel and Ramsey

were mobilised. The fire was quickly extinguished, but a major gas leak occurred because the the damaged valve could not be closed. About 11am, 25 minutes after the first incident, DCO Hopkins confirmed that the major incident plan should be put into operation.

The police requested people to evacuate property on the South Quay and spray jets were placed in strategic positions. Other out-of-town stations were alerted and placed on stand-by. By noon 44 firemen were at the scene. The leak had been partly sealed but it was not until 3.30pm that the damaged valves were removed and the pipes blanked off. The escaping gas had been able to vent safely within the harbour, which had been closed to shipping. The wind direction had blown the gas towards the mouth of the harbour, away from the town. The fire service stood down at 5.15pm and most of the population of Douglas had been unaware how close they had come to a major explosion.

In 1988 there was a different gas problem. For three years, complaints had been made about alleged gas leaks around Granville Street. All had been investigated by the gas company, and nothing found. During March there had been a significant increase in complaints, particularly in the cellars of the Rio Hotel. The fire brigade made several attendances and eventually found flammable gas using portable detection equipment.

On Saturday March 26, Douglas Corporation officials investigated the pump chambers of a sewage ejector station in Granville Street. They broke up the footway adjoining the Rio Hotel to release trapped gas under the highway. Gas readings continued to rise on the Sunday, so electricity and gas supplies were disconnected to the Rio and the El Cortez hotels to minimise the risk of explosion. Tests on the gas main in Granville Street detected nothing.

During Monday the street was sealed and drainage engineers from the Department of Highways, Ports and Properties used closed circuit TV equipment and found damage in a pipe leading from the pneumatic sewage ejector. The underground ejector chamber was again entered; disused ejectors were inspected and found to contain old raw sewage which had generated biological methane. The gas had found its way through damaged pipes into the surrounding ground and the basements of the properties. Natural ventilation relieved the immediate problem but the remedial work was to take many weeks.

The fire brigade attended on and off for more than a week, in particular during the following Saturday and Sunday. With flammable gas readings of 80 per cent in the basements of the hotels, and 100 per cent in the manholes in the back yards, the fire brigade had recommended evacuation. The owners were reluctant to leave; this presented a dilemma for the fire service and the police, who lacked at that time any statutory powers. In the event, evacuation was completed by Sunday night.

In May 1988, a severe fire occurred in premises at Merton Bank occupied by BP Joinery. Two calls were received at control, the first from the proprietor of La Cucina restaurant and the second from harbour control at the Sea Terminal — both around midnight on May 7. Five pumps and the turntable ladder were quickly in attendance with six jets, turntable ladder monitor and ground monitor in use. Sub-officer Cliffe and fireman Howland were the first to enter the building. They were progressing to the seat of the fire with a branch when a flash-over occurred, forcing their immediate withdrawal and resulting in the whole building, a former church hall, being engulfed in fire.

An old peoples' home in Demesne Road backed onto the fire ground; radiated heat broke glass in rear windows and activated smoke alarms, resulting in the safe evacuation of the residents. The point of interest was that the smoke detectors responded to a fire outside the building, once again underlining their value.

A number of fires towards the end of 1990 involved elderly people, with regrettably tragic consequences. In one incident in Castletown, a passer-by heard the alarm going off inside a building. He called the brigade, but was too late to save the elderly person inside. The incident did, however, emphasise the value of smoke detectors, particularly for elderly persons living alone. They can attract the attention of neighbours in the event of fire. These instances led to the Chief Fire Officer, John Hinnigan, issuing a Christmas message: "Hear smoke with a smoke detector."

Douglas had operated a foam tender/hose carrier for a number of years, starting with a Green Goddess transferred from Castletown to Douglas in 1977 and carrying foam in drums. This was followed by an F8, also from Castletown, which carried foam in the water tank. Finally there was an F28, originally stationed in Douglas but at Castletown from 1984, and converted in the brigade workshops to a foam tender/specialised appliance in 1988.

With the increased storage of fuel and gas at Douglas, it was time to consider a purpose-built appliance to meet the various demands of the service. The new appliance arrived in the summer of 1988, built by Nova Scotia of Blackburn on a three-axle Volvo FL10 chassis. It carried 30 lengths of hose, which could be laid on the run, and an independently Fiat-powered 900gpm Coventry Climax pump which enabled the vehicle to discharge 1,200gpm of foam through a centrally-mounted Kerr monitor on the run.

The same pump could, if necessary, be used for relay pumping in remote rural areas. It was designed to carry 1,000 gallons of water, 300 gallons of high expansion foam and 300 gallons of low-expansion foam. Foam generation was through an Ess mixer with a 400 gallon water capacity, giving a total generated capacity of 2,400gpm of foam. This enabled full delivery through the monitor and two branches, through a variety of discharge methods. Although large, the appliance has proved very versatile.

Later in the same year, the old turntable ladder was replaced by a 30-metre four-section Metz ladder supplied by Angloco on a Volvo FL6 chassis. The ladder was the first on the Island capable of working to 17° below the horizontal and with a maximum elevation of 75°. The head of the ladder was fitted for cage operation; this allowed the fireman at the head of the ladder to operate the monitor from above the source of fire, giving him protection from radiated heat. The appliance was supplied with a 500gpm pump and the usual equipment, at a cost of £247,620.

During 1988 the service was renamed The Isle of Man Fire and Rescue Service. In accordance with government policy, this name appeared on a number of appliances — in Manx Gaelic as well as English.

The turntable ladder turned out to its first call at a fire on a

Dennis F46A PWT, from Douglas station, tackling a fire at the Douglas Motorcycle Centre in September 1982. The ERF hydraulic platform enabled the men to reach the seat of the blaze.

demolition site at the former Douglas Bay Hotel. The hose-laying vehicle was also used, as water had to be relayed at this area notorious for poor water pressure. The fire was severe but did not endanger any other property. Nevertheless, five pumps were required and three ground monitors were also used, in addition to the monitors on the turntable ladder and hydraulic platform.

The brigade became concerned at this time about the number of fires carelessly started on demolition sites. There had been serious fires to contend with at the Peveril Hotel site and the Regal Cinema site where adjoining property was put at risk. Two incidents occurred at Ramsey, where building work resulted in spread of fire and the eventual demolition of the properties involved. This led to the Fire Prevention Department, in conjunction with the Health and Safety Inspectorate, insisting on proper precautions being taken by demolition contractors.

In 1989, following extensive evaluation of numerous all-terrain vehicles, the first of a new breed of appliances was introduced to replace the aging Land Rovers at the out-stations. The requirement was for a small, compact vehicle capable of getting up narrow country and farm lanes, which also had good road speed, could carry its own water and be able to service the town and village districts.

The appliance that arrived did all that the old Land Rovers did and more. Built by Saxon on the Steyr Daimler Puch Pinzgauer 6 x 6 chassis, and powered by a 2.3 litre turbo diesel engine, it carried a five-man crew, three breathing sets, 200 gallons of water, a 350gpm Godiva pump with two deliveries also capable of being removed from the vehicle, a standard hose reel and a 10.5 metre Angus/Sarol triple extension ladder. After further trials by full-time personnel it was allocated to Peel, replacing the 1964 Land Rover. Two more of these appliances were immediately ordered. The first was stationed at Ramsey during 1990 and the second, manufactured by Mountain Range, was scheduled to be stationed at Castletown, replacing the Austin Gypsy.

On August 28, 1989, the Island lost another of its traditional timber-built cafés left over from the Victorian era. At 4.22am a call was received at fire control reporting that the Waterfall Café at Glenmaye was on fire. Peel brigade was alerted and had its first appliance at Glenmaye ten minutes later, followed by the Douglas appliances some eight minutes after that, manned by the full-time duty crew. That was 18 minutes from the call being logged to arrival at the fire ground, almost ten miles from Douglas: a very creditable performance.

Even so, they were still too late to save the café. The timber building was gutted and severely damaged, eventually having to be demolished. The stop call came only 20 minutes after arrival, three jets and breathing apparatus having been used on the fire.

The end of the decade saw yet more appliances being delivered as part of the progressive modernisation programme. Early in 1990 a Fulton-Wylie-built tender ladder on a Volvo FL614 chassis was delivered to become the first-call appliance for Douglas. Narrower than the Dennis it replaced, it had a six-man crew cab, a 1,000gpm Godiva pump with four deliveries, carried 400 gallons of water, 200 litres of high expansion foam, two high pressure hose reels, a selection of ladders (the largest being a 15-metre Angus/Sarol) and all the usual hand tools, including a Black Hawk hydraulic cutter, reflecting the increasing number of road accidents to which the brigade has to respond.

Despite being a narrow appliance, it still had difficulty getting to the scene of a serious fire in Castle Mona Avenue on March 3, 1990. A call was received shortly before 3am, reporting a fire in the Aston Ville, a residential hotel, with people trapped on upper floors. The cul-de-sac behind the central promenade is notorious for parked vehicles. The first appliance collided with a parked car and was slightly damaged. The fire was serious and the call was for "pumps four" and the turntable ladder. There were found to be 21 people in the hotel, and access to the three-storey rear outlet was difficult.

Laxey, Castletown, Peel and Kirk Michael brigades were alerted; at the height of the fire, six pumps and the turntable ladder were in use and ten breathing sets used by the firemen. Eleven people were rescued by ladder from the front and rear of the building, one of whom was taken to hospital suffering cuts, burns and smoke inhalation. The problems of access caused by indiscriminate parking in residential areas remains a problem for the brigade, despite meetings involving the police and others.

Another 4 x 4 appliance was delivered later in the year and allocated to Douglas, giving the station a modern, purpose-built all-wheel drive vehicle. Bigger than those at the out-stations, it was supplied by Carmichael on a Mercedes 917 chassis with a six-man crew cab. It carried 300 gallons of water and 100 litres of foam, delivery being through a 500gpm pump. In addition to the usual hand equipment, it carried a 10.5 metre triple Angus/Sarol ladder, four breathing sets and a high-pressure hose reel.

In the last decade the fire service has substituted, or added, 15 new appliances to its fleet, together with van and car replacements. The manning level of the brigade has increased by 20 and the fire prevention section has been increased to enable the requirements of the Fire Precautions Act 1975 and its subsequent orders and regulations to be enforced, including the inspection of all plans submitted for planning approval.

9. Private brigades

The airport fire service and others

DETAILS of the Island's private fire brigades are scarce. The first was without doubt the Sun Insurance Brigade which has already been adequately described because of its place in the development of organised fire fighting within the Island.

The next brigade was formed at King William's College following the destructive fire of 1844. It stemmed from the need for self-preservation and included masters and boys.

They acquired second-hand equipment from time to time from the regular brigades. After mains water was installed at the college, the brigade operated with hose and standpipes from the various hydrants within the grounds. At one time two of the old street escapes from Douglas saw service there.

Some years before Castletown had a motor fire engine there was a fire at the college which was first tackled by its own brigade. It was soon joined by the Castletown Brigade, which lost no time in summoning help from Douglas. The Leyland was dispatched and eventually the fire was put out.

The Douglas men telephoned their chief to say that they were returning to station, and left the college. Some two hours later he became concerned because his men had not returned. Fearing the worst he set off in search of them. It was a clear moonlit night at Douglas and he could not understand the delay. He met them at the top of Richmond Hill; they were tired, cold and wet.

Snow had started to fall shortly after they had left the college and it took them an hour and a half to get up Ballaglonney hill, manhandling first the appliance and then the trailer pump. For the rest of the time they sat on the outside of the appliance, exposed to the elements.

The college later acquired the Bean engine which had seen service in various parts of the Island. In the mid 1950s the Civil Defence Commission loaned the 1939 ex-Ramsey Morris to the college brigade, and a garage was built to house it. It remained in use at the college for almost 20 years being replaced by a Bedford Green Goddess, also on loan from the Commission and still in service at the college.

James Moore, agent to the Sun Fire Office in 1801, formed the local Sun Insurance Brigade. When the Sun withdrew its service, James Moore's son William was the agent. He purchased the small manual fire engine in 1848 for use in his sailcloth works at Tromode.

It is known from contemporary reports that William Moore had a number of trained men capable of firefighting and operating the fire engine, and that it was still in use some ten years later.

In 1867, a lunatic asylum was completed at the Strang, almost three miles from Douglas. It accommodated 76 patients, the number soon increasing three-fold. The asylum had its own gas-producing plant, laundry and steam-pumping arrangements for its water supply, which was taken from wells and underground rain water tanks.

The building represented a high fire risk, notably because of the presence of a system of timber ventilating ducts serving Howorth's Patent Ventilating System.

By 1870 the maintenance staff and the attendants had formed a fire brigade under the charge of the clerk of works. In 1876 two L'Extincteur patent fire extinguishers were purchased and the medical superintendent, Dr T O Wood, recommended the installation of external hydrants. An outbreak of fire in the female division in 1882 prompted the installation of an external main and hydrants, complete with steam force pumps to pressurise the system.

The asylum fire brigade was in action at 6.45am on February 5, 1891, after an attendant accidentally set fire to the proscenium curtain and staging in the dining room while lighting the gas lamps. The Sun Insurance Company met the repair costs.

Between 1901 and 1902 the Asylum Board renewed all the pillar hydrants and installed internal hydrants with lengths of hose supplied by Wm Rose & Co and incorporating their instantaneous couplings. The asylum had underground water storage of 19,000 gallons, with header tanks of 4,000 gallon capacity but, even with steam force, the pressure was inadequate for efficient fire-fighting as it was impossible to throw a jet of water over the highest building. The situation was remedied in 1904 when terms were agreed with Douglas Corporation to take a four-inch supply off the main town supply which had been laid from the new Baldwin Reservoir.

This mains water supply was fed into the existing asylum system and the pressure was sufficient to throw a jet over the ridge of the three-storey dormitories.

In 1907 the asylum brigade was called to a fire outside the grounds in a cottage at the Strang belonging to a Mrs Corkill. The fire had threatened the stack-yard belonging to the asylum, but was quickly and efficiently extinguished.

The influx of internees to the Island, and a tremendous increase in the number of inmates, presented further problems for the asylum. Accommodation for the poor was built adjoining the asylum, so there were now some 500 persons under the care of the Asylum Board. Fire prevention had never been more important.

The brigade was completely reorganised in 1917 and a simple set of rules printed. Arrangements were made for Douglas fire brigade to give demonstrations and hold regular drills with the asylum brigade.

In 1922 one of the main fire hazards at the asylum — now known as the Mental Hospital — was removed with the installation of a generator and conversion to electric lighting.

The Asylum Board had continued the training of both male and female hospital attendants; regular drills were conducted by the Superintendent of the Douglas Brigade. However, Douglas had now acquired its first motor fire engine and it could be in attendance at the hospital ten minutes after leaving the station. This radically altered the situation at the hospital. In order to meet the demands of the motor pump, one of the rainwater tanks in the basement was connected to the mains supply and used as a static tank. The Leyland engine could then be fed with a good supply of water and a jet thrown over the central tower.

The staff at the hospital continued to drill regularly and provided an efficient first-aid cover. They extinguished many small fires within the hospital and the Home of the Poor, later known as the Infirmary. In 1935 additional mains and hydrants were provided and extra hose acquired.

During the second world war a fire party was maintained, despite many of the young nursing staff and maintenance staff serving in the armed forces. A Merryweather Warspite pump powered by a twin Anzani engine was stationed at the hospital for use in the event of a mains failure.

The fire party, made up mostly from maintenance and ancillary staff under the direction of the clerk of works, was finally disbanded in 1986.

The hospital is still a high-risk building; following the 1975 Fire Precautions Act, heat and smoke detectors were fitted in all the buildings, with a direct link to the Automatic Fire Alarm Panel at Central Fire Control in Douglas.

Mention has been made of the numerous fire parties formed during the second world war, many loosely falling into the category of private fire brigades. Most were not part of the AFS set-up although they did attend training courses and combined exercises from time to time. Notable examples were the fire parties formed by Marks & Spencer, Boots and Nobles Hospital. The branches of the national multiple stores had implemented an overall policy on fire-watching which had become compulsory in the UK following the London blitz. There was, however, no such legal requirement in the Isle of Man.

Some of the military establishments had fire parties mainly made up from civilian personnel. One such party operated at the Royal Naval Sick Quarters at the Children's Home on Glencrutchery Road which was attached to *HMS St George*.

Fire at sea

Vessels of the IoM Steam Packet Company, and other shipping companies operating out of the Island, come under the jurisdiction of subordinate legislation of the UK having effect in the Isle of Man. The Merchant Shipping (Fire Appliances) Rules, 1965, and its 1974 amendment, lay down stringent safety rules enforced by the Department of Trade and Industry. Each vessel is required to have fire parties and to hold regular drills; inspections are made annually by officials of the department.

The fire-prevention equipment they carry varies from ship to ship, although the principle is essentially the same. Car ferries, for example, are fitted with Mather & Platt Grinnel automatic sprinkler systems designed to operate when the temperature under the sprinkler heads reaches 68°C. The vessels are divided into eight drencher sections with central control valves and port and starboard shore connections to supplement the on-board fire-fighting equipment. An automatic fire alarm panel is linked to the system and located in the wheelhouse, together with a smoke detector indicator panel.

Alarm and communication systems are opened from the wheelhouse, and emergency procedures to compartment the ship are also indicated there. Fire parties are made up of the engineering staff, crew and the ship's carpenter under under the direction of an officer. The vessels have a comprehensive hydrant and hose-reel system, and the steam-operated vessels had separate foam boiler-room drench systems. Vessels are also equipped with Siebe Gorman smoke helmets with trailing air lines connected to hand bellows, giving the fire parties limited access to smoke-logged areas.

The Isle of Man Fire Service undergoes familiarisation drills with various vessels, to acquaint personnel with ship layout and shore connections. A number of minor outbreaks, mostly confined to ships' lounges, have been dealt with while vessels were berthed overnight at Douglas.

The earliest incident involving a vessel of the IoM Steam Packet Company occurred at Liverpool on June 12, 1847. The *SS King Orry*, berthed at the landing stage, blew a boiler plug and required the attendance of the Liverpool City Fire Brigade. One man was injured in the boiler room, though the efforts of the crew and the fire brigade ensured there was no permanent damage.

The Douglas brigade was called to a fire on board the *SS Mona* in May 1928; an account for £19 17s was rendered, but other details are tantalisingly scarce. More recently the fire service was called to a fire in a linen store on board the *SS Manxman*. Fire at sea is possibly the most difficult situation to confront fire-fighting personnel. Responsibility initially rests upon the ship's fire party, but urgent help is a priority if the fire is too large to be contained.

Conscious of its strategic position in the Irish Sea, the Isle of Man Fire Service has recently set up a procedure with the Coastguard and RAF Valley in Anglesey for getting aid to any ship on fire. Regular exercises are held in conjunction with the lifeboat service. Equipment is preloaded into purpose-made canvas bags, enabling it to be handled quickly and easily into Wessex helicopters; in addition to personnel these can carry suction-hose and lightweight pump.

Exercises have also been undertaken with tugs belonging to the Laxey Towing Company. While these vessels are primarily harbour tugs, they do have a reasonable sea-going ability. They also have built-in salvage pumps; in one case a monitor is mounted aft of the funnel. Supplemented by portable pumps and monitors, the Island fire service now has an afloat capability. Three jets have been discharged simultaneously from the tug *Union*, reaching a height of 70 feet.

During preparations for the second world war, the Central Air Raids Precautions Committee was concerned about the effects of gas warfare, so anti-gas precautions were introduced in 1939 by the Harbour Board. A decontamination squad was set up in each port, with personnel recruited from harbour police and harbour masters.

In December 1941 the Harbour Board acquired the Dodge fire tender from the Laxey Fire Authority for decontamination duties and to provide additional fire cover for Douglas harbour. It was parked during the period of the war by the Edward Pier viaduct and manned by the Harbour Board employees as required. At the end of hostilities it was broken up.

Airport cover

Regular air services between the Island and the United Kingdom began in the early 1930s, and the first regular airport was established on fields at Ronaldsway farm in the south of the Island. A service was established by the Blackpool and West Coast Air Services Ltd, and regular flights began in June 1933. Soon De Havilland DH84s, and other aircraft, were using the airfield.

On Monday July 1, 1935, a twin-engine De Havilland Dragon, operated for Manx Airways by Railway Air Services, began take-off. At the end of the 700-yard runway it became airborne, but as it fought to gain height the undercarriage caught in the wire of the airport boundary fence. The pilot, Captain Pierce, fought to regain control, crossing the field adjacent to the airport, but the aircraft hit the next hedge and nose-dived into a potato field. Two passengers were thrown out on impact; despite being dazed they set about rescuing the other four passengers and the pilot. The starboard engine had caught fire but the occupants managed to get out before the fire spread to the fabric of the plane.

Mr Mason, the airport manager, telephoned for the police and the fire brigade. The brigade was despatched from Douglas; though quickly at the scene it was unable to save the plane.

The ambulance was also despatched from Nobles Hospital and made two journeys between Ronaldsway and Douglas. Captain Pierce and a passenger, a Mrs Teare from Ballagaraghyn, were detained in hospital. The brigade account for the service was £14.

After an inquiry, by two Inspectors from the Air Ministry, the airfield had to provide its own fire-fighting cover. The Blackpool and West Coast Company acquired a 12hp Morris van from a Port Erin confectioner and converted it to a fire tender. The work was carried out by its own ground staff; they removed the van body and fitted a rack to the chassis to take three Pyrene foam extinguisher bottles, giving Ronaldsway its first airport fire tender.

As an aside to this incident, the ambulance from Nobles Hospital which was used at the crash was acquired for airfield use at Ronaldsway in 1950.

A second airport operated between 1935 and 1937 in the north of the Island, on fields at Close Lake Farm, Andreas. Scant records indicate, however, that the only fire-fighting equipment was a small trolley-mounted portable fire extinguisher.

With the advent of war, Ronaldsway was acquired by the British Government and additional land purchased. Three tarmac runways and associated hangarage were built and, in the winter of 1939-40, Ronaldsway became a Royal Air Force training station.

In 1942 the RAF transferred to a newly established aerodrome in the north of the Island, and Ronaldsway was handed over to the Admiralty. It established a training station as part of the Fleet Air Arm and named it *HMS Urley*. The West Coast company was allowed to operate a restricted service out of Ronaldsway, with fire cover provided by the Royal Naval Air Service. The station operated Barracuda aircraft, fire cover being provided by duty crash crews using three crash tenders.

The main appliance was a Crossley FE1 6 x 4 with a 300-gallon water tank and a 28-gallon foam liquid tank. Foam was generated by a foam-entraining perforated impeller pump with a single hose delivery. In addition, four carbon dioxide bottles were carried on the side of the vehicle.

The second foam tender was a Fordson WOT 1 standard wartime appliance, also on a 6 x 4 chassis and carrying 300 gallons of water, but with 100 gallons of foam. Delivery was through two hose sidelines off a pump identical to the Crossley. CO_2 could also be discharged from four 60lb cylinders through 75ft of $^3/_4$" hose.

The third appliance was a four-wheel conventional drive Austin fire tender with a 1,000gpm Tangye pump and four deliveries. It also towed a 100gpm trailer pump, all equipped for water only.

In 1939 the RAF began work on a permanent station at Jurby, in the north of the Island. Eventually two tarmac runways were built and hangarage for 70 Anson aircraft, on the condition that RAF Jurby became an air navigation school under Flying Training Command.

Less than five miles away a temporary aerodrome with three runways was opened in August 1941 at Andreas. RAF Andreas

The Airport Fire Service's Jet Ranger 2000, built by Carmichael and powered by a Detroit 12-litre engine. Pictured alongside is a Carmichael Rapid Intervention Vehicle, based on the Range Rover.

was initially a fighter station, its role being the defence of shipping using the north channel and the ports of Belfast, Liverpool and Glasgow. Later it came under the Flying Training Command as No11 Air Gunnery School. Martinets, Wellingtons and Spitfires regularly used the airfield.

Both stations had the standard allocation of a Crossley and Fordson, similar to those at Ronaldsway. The normal procedure was for the crash tenders to be stationed alongside the control tower while the station was operational, returning to the compound on stand-down.

The worst incident of the war occurred at Jurby; although no

lives were lost, the damage was extensive. During May 1945 a Sunderland flying boat with one engine on fire made a forced landing on the airfield. It was carrying eight ariel mines and was successfully brought down. The station had been evacuated of all but essential personnel, because of this dangerous cargo.

The crash crew tried to tackle the fire, which had spread to the wing, but it was too well established. Because of the mines, they were ordered to retreat. The Sunderland blew up and almost every window on the camp was broken. The roofs of the main hangers were severely damaged, and the crash crew had little else to do but damp down small fires around the airfield.

Later, in September, a fire broke out in the stack-yard at Ballalough Farm, Andreas. The fire was extinguished by the RAF Andreas fire service; the men were unable to save the 20-ton stack, but at least they stopped the fire spreading to the adjoining buildings. Shortly after this incident Andreas aerodrome closed down.

Jurby continued after hostilities as a training and operational aerodrome. The Crossley was replaced by a military version of the Thornycroft/Pyrene Mk V, and the Fordson by a Thornycroft dual-purpose tender with a large water-carrying capacity. It served as a back-up vehicle and carried an extension ladder; it had sidelines for domestic fires on airfield property.

A personnel rescue vehicle was also stationed at Jurby in the late 1950s. It echoed the wartime experience of getting people out of a crashed plane quickly where converted jeeps or similar vehicles had been used for the purpose.

Now it was purpose-built, based on a Land Rover chassis and carrying two dry-powder extinguishers discharged by compressed nitrogen through two hose deliveries stowed flaked on side racks. The vehicle also carried a stalk light and other emergency gear.

During 1946 and 1947 Ronaldsway was operated by the Ministry of Civil Aviation. Then, in March 1948, the airport was bought by the Isle of Man Government for £11,500, shortly after the Isle of Man Airports Board was formed. The fire appliances and the two crash crews were part of the deal.

Ronaldsway, operating under the new Board, soon found the wartime appliances unable to make long road journeys. This gave the Board a problem as it had obtained permission to use Jurby as a diversionary airport in the event of fog or cross-winds, and a condition of its use was that it should provide its own fire cover.

To overcome the problem the old Leyland was loaned to the Airports Board by the Douglas Corporation. Stripped of its wheeled escape and accessories, but still with its pump and hose-reel, it took up its duties on September 11, 1948. The airport fire service was at this time made up on a part-time basis with members of the fire crew working also as baggage-handlers,

porters and maintenance staff.

During 1953, Mr Mayall, Chief Fire Staff Officer, was instructed by the Local Government Board at the request of the Airports Board to advise on the airport fire service arrangements and to assist in training. Prior to this, one appliance was housed in a small fire station under the control tower, with the remainder in one of the hangers. The aircraft on regular service were becoming larger; Dakotas predominated, with occasional Ambassadors (*Elizabethans*), Doves and Herons.

Mr Mayall could clearly see the need for a drastic re-organisation of the airport fire service. During the following year he undertook 72 lecture sessions, including practical training, on fighting aircraft fires. He also arranged for Castletown and Ramsey Brigades to exercise with the Airport Fire Service.

When a major fault developed in the Austin's foam pump, the Airport Board was left with no alternative but to order a replacement.

The new appliance was a 40 HP Thornycroft/Pyrene Mk V foam tender based on the Nubian 4 x 4 chassis; it entered service in July 1955. For the first time the crew was accommodated within a fully enclosed cab. The appliance carried 550 gallons of water and 50 gallons of foam compound. Foam could be discharged through a roof monitor with the vehicle stationary and from two four-inch deliveries either side. Water could be discharged through two rear deliveries. It was the first Mk V to be delivered to a civil airport in the UK.

During 1958 the Airports Board continued to improve the fire section, adopting International Civil Aviation Regulations. Mr Mayall continued to train the crash crews, conducting a further series of lectures and exercises with members of Castletown and Ramsey brigades for appliance familiarisation. Crews at RAF Jurby were joined in similar exercises by Ramsey and Kirk Michael brigades.

In June, a full-scale exercise was staged, involving all units. Following the lessons learned, a scheme for dealing with a major air crash outside the airport limits was drawn up and codenamed Operation Hillsearch.

In September a diesel engined dual-purpose appliance based

on a Ford Thames Trader chassis was introduced. It carried 800 gallons of water and 75 gallons of foam with two side deliveries on each side through a Coventry Climax 600gpm pump, foam being aspirated at the branch.

To bring the airport fire section up to date a rapid intervention vehicle based on an Austin Gypsy was introduced in May 1959. It was fitted with dry-powder cylinders discharged by CO_2 through two 27ft hose deliveries. It carried a full set of electrically operated cutting tools and a small folding ladder.

In 1960 Vickers Viscount turbo-prop aircraft were introduced on regular service flights to Ronaldsway. Fire section facilities had to be improved.

The section leader, Mr Arthur Corlett, who had been in charge of the crash crew since 1946, attended the first of many training courses organised through the Civil Aviation Authority Fire School at Rhoose Airport, Cardiff. Mr R W C Corkish was appointed as deputy and he too attended similar courses. After completing basic training, the fire section was reorganised using the same ranking system as in the rest of the UK and Mr Corlett became the station officer.

To provide additional cover a second-hand war department 30 HP Austin 4 x 6 CO_2 fire tender was acquired. It carried 24 bottles of CO_2 in four racks, amounting to a total capacity of 1,440 lbs of gas at a pressure of 800psi. Discharge was through two 75ft lengths of $3/_4$" hose and long-handled applicators. The appliance was bought in June 1960 and reconditioned in the airport's own motor transport section; it entered service soon afterwards.

The airport was modernised at the same time. The improvements included a new three-bay station built adjacent to the east apron. The fire station moved into the new premises in March 1961; for the first time the crash crew and appliances were all housed together adjacent to the main terminal area. All appliances were fitted with radio and put in direct contact with Air Traffic Control.

In 1964 the RAF ceased operations at Jurby; Operation Hillsearch ended with the withdrawal of skilled personnel. The Isle of Man Government bought Jurby to use as a diversionary airport, and extended the main runway to accommodate Vis-

counts. Fire cover was provided by the Airport Fire Service whenever the airfield was used, usually with the old Fordson and an appliance from the Ramsey Brigade. An additional dual-purpose appliance was bought for Ronaldsway in January 1965. It was based on a Bedford chassis with the same bodywork pump and equipment as the Thames dual-purpose appliance.

Runway extensions were made at Ronaldsway during 1970 to allow the introduction of BAC 1-11 series 400 jet aircraft. At the same time the Airport Fire Service took delivery of an 18ft inshore lifeboat powered by a 40 HP Evinrude outboard motor. The boat was acquired to apply with International Regulations as three of the airport's main runway approaches are over the sea. The boat was trailer-mounted and towed by the Gypsy, extending its role as a rapid intervention vehicle.

All fire crew personnel were now regularly attending courses at the CAA fire school, although the training base had moved to Stansted. As part of the continuing need to modernise the service, the Airports Board embarked yet again on a change of equipment.

A major foam tender was acquired in January 1973, the largest ever to be introduced in the Island up to that date. It was a Thornycroft Nubian Mk II based on a three-axle chassis powered by a 15 litre 300bhp Cummins V-8 engine. Carrying 1,400 gallons of water and 140 gallons of foam, it had an all-up weight of 20 tons.

The appliance was the first on the airport capable of discharging foam on the move, through a fully controllable roof-mounted monitor at a rate of 7,000gpm. In addition to the roof monitor the appliance carries side deliveries for foam and water and a rear-mounted first aid hose reel. Branches, tools and hose are carried in side lockers and a Bristol reflectorised fire-fighting suit, helmet and boots is carried in the crew cab together with breathing apparatus.

The modernisation programme was completed in 1979 with the addition of two further appliances. At this time the vehicles were numbered and given call signs and lettered out of the side panels as Ronaldsway Aerodrome Fire Service, all vehicles carrying UHF radio.

The first of the two appliances arrived in March. It was a rapid-intervention vehicle built by Carmichael and based on a 6 x 4 Range Rover chassis. Designed mainly for personnel rescue, it carries 200 gallons of light water premix discharged through a roof monitor and 92kgs of BCF liquid, a halogenated fire-extinguishing agent, through a nitrogen pressurised hose reel.

The appliance is designated *Fire One* and is the first-call appliance, carrying full cutting gear, small ladder and Bristol suit. The total discharge time for the fire fighting agents carried is 90 seconds, during which time any rescue has to be effected although the back-up foam equipment is very close behind. The standard of firemanship of the crew and knowledge of entry into aircraft has to be of an extremely high standard.

The second appliance arrived in October and cost £80,000. It was a Jet Ranger 2000 major foam unit, built by Carmichael, on a specialist chassis from Shelvoke and Drewery, powered by a 12-litre turbo-charged V8 Detroit diesel engine of 430 bhp, giving a top speed of 50mph. The appliance carries 1,800 gallons of water and 200 gallons of FP 570 foam compound and, like the Nubian, discharges foam at the rate of 7,000gpm through a controllable roof monitor fed by a 1,200gpm Godiva Mk 14 pump. Side foam deliveries at 1,000gpm are similar to the Nubian, but the hose reel is mounted on the offside. The normal crew complement is three, with the driver and monitor operator linked by internal intercom. The operational weight of 22 tons now makes it the largest appliance on the Island.

The Jet Ranger was allocated the call sign *Fire 2*, the Nubian *Fire 3* and the Bedford, dating from 1965, *Fire 4*. The brigade complement was 14 firemen in two seven-man watches under a Station Officer, Deputy and section leader. A continuous training programme is undertaken with wet and dry drills, and frequent combined exercises with the Island Fire Service for appliance familiarisation.

The Airport Fire Service operates under comprehensive operational orders and procedures, with predetermined attendance to all locations on the airport. For a full emergency turnout at Ronaldsway there is a predetermined reinforcement scheme involving the Island Fire Service with attendance by two major pumps from Castletown, a major pump, hose-carrier and emergency tender from Douglas and a pump escape from Port Erin.

Fire 2 and *Fire 3* have a complete foam discharge time of just over two minutes each, so that any aircraft fire has to be knocked out and smothered within that time to be effective. Again, this requires a high degree of skill.

To produce foam the major units require a vast amount of water. As the airport has no water ring main, the additional manpower and pumping capacity provided by the reinforcement scheme is essential for relay pumping from the five static water tanks, storing 132,000 gallons within the airport boundary. Foam blankets are no longer laid as they are considered to be inefficient.

A reciprocal arrangement exists with operation Oil Fire, in which *Fire 3* would be immediately sent to Douglas as a reinforcing appliance in the event of a fire occurring in the main petroleum fuel storage depot.

The fire section provides cover on the airport apron as required, using portable BCF 25lb wheeled extinguishers with long-handled applicators.

In 1986 the former Isle of Man Airports Board became part of the Department of Highways, Ports and Properties, with its fire vehicles being maintained at the central plant depot at Crosby. The airport soon embarked on an improvement scheme which was to be phased over a number of years; one of the first problems to be addressed was the fire section.

Personnel were increased to 22, made up from one station officer, one deputy fire officer, two section leaders and 18 firemen. A watch consists of one section leader and six firemen. A new site was determined for the Airport Fire Station and it was built near to the old barn site on the opposite side of the airfield to the terminal building. From this modern five-bay station, with full messing facilities and a modern control room located at roof level, the duty watchman could now for the first time command a view of the whole airfield. The station was opened on Monday, 21 May, 1990, by the Chief Minister, the Hon Miles Walker MHK.

The same day saw the DHPP take delivery of a replacement for *Fire 4*. Just as Ronaldsway had been the first airport to receive

The fire brigade provides emergency lighting as a Wessex helicopter from RAFVAlley airlifts a boy injured in a cliff fall to Walton Hospital Liverpool, in 1982. The landing site is in King George V Park, to the rear of the fire station.

a civilian Thornycroft/Pyrene Mk V, so this new appliance was to be an all-time first. Manufactured by Simon Gloster Saro and built on a 4 x 4 Mercedes Benz 1936 AF-38 chassis, the new airport crash-rescue vehicle was the first of the Defender series.

It carries 4,500 litres of water and 540 litres of foam, delivery being through a roof monitor at a discharge rate of 2,300 litres/minute over a distance of 50 metres through 135 degrees of rotation. There are also two foam sidelines, two water branches and a first-aid hose-reel. Foam generation is through a centrifugal unit powered by a Godiva UFPX Mk 14 pump. The appliance can also deliver 100kg of Halon 1211 powder through a sideline. For night work, illumination is provided by a Clark TF mast carrying 2 x 1,000 Watt floodlights. The standard Mercedes cab provides accommodation for a crew of five and the appliance can accelerate to 50mph in 40 seconds with an all-up weight in excess of 16 tonnes.

Pictured, left, is a Bedford Green Goddess, acquired by the Civil Defence Commission in 1968. It is pictured outside the central fire station in 1986, while on loan to King William's College. The striking architectural style of the the fire station is shown in the other picture.

The new appliance proved its value in December 1990 when a Manx Airlines British Aerospace Advanced Turbo Prop careered off the runway after its nose-wheel collapsed on landing. The airport fire service was mobilised immediately and reached the aircraft before the engines were shut down. Fortunately there was no fire and the 70 passengers were evacuated without injury by the aircrew through the front passenger door.

Two branch lines were run out from *Fire 3* and the aircraft checked for fuel leaks. Appliances from Castletown, Douglas and Port Erin attended the incident but were not required. Retrieval of the aircraft was achieved with some difficulty, illumination and cover being provided by the airport fire service.

A programme of vehicle replacement and refurbishment began with Fire 5 being replaced by a Toyota 4 x 4 vehicle from within the Department's vehicle fleet, its normal duties being for inspection, bird-scaring and towing the inshore rescue boat. *Fire 3* received a comprehensive refit, extending its useful life by 20 years. All the airport appliances changed their livery from red to yellow, and during 1990 all appliances adopted the new airport logo "The airport, Isle of Man". *Fire 2* was sent for a similar refit towards the end of the year, after which the airport fire service would have a modern station equipped with completely updated appliances.

During the winter of 1979/80 the Auxiliary Fire Service was reconstituted by the Civil Defence Commission, and Mr R A Christian was appointed officer in charge. The AFS now has a strength of eight and operates the two remaining Bedford Green Goddess appliances. These were due to be supplemented by the Dennis F28 on its replacement by the new DS series Dennis, stationed at Laxey.

The Austin CO_2 tender which the Airport Fire Service acquired in 1960 became surplus to requirements when the new appliances were delivered in 1979. It was quickly snapped up by a new company, Thermo Skyships, which had started building airships at Jurby airfield. The company had to provide cover for its activities and to enable its use of the airfield. This elderly appliance saw several years of service at Jurby before being preserved in the Imperial War Museum.

The company, now called the Advanced Airship Corporation Ltd, has continued to expand and, with its first flight planned for 1991, has provided fire cover since 1988 with a Land Rover based appliance. At present it can only discharge water through two sidelines and carries 50 gallons of water with a further 200 gallons in a coupled trailer. The vehicle is to be modified to carry and discharge foam and is manned by the company workforce.

Appendices

i. LIST OF PREMISES USED AS FIRE STATIONS

DOUGLAS
1860-1862 Douglas Court House, Church Street.
1862- Collister's Yard, Athol Street
-1869 Hampton's Yard
1869-1874 Commissioners Yard, Fort Street
1874- Hills Brewery, Hills Estate
- 1900 Thos Moore's Livery Stable, Circular Road
1900- 1977 Municipal Buildings, John Street
1977- Peel Road

DOUGLAS No 2 STATION
1935-1977 Lord Street

PEEL
1885-1895 Rocket Brigade House.
1895-1921 Station Road
1921-1941 Boilley Spittall
1941-1968 Market Square
1968- Queen's Drive

RAMSEY
1887-1889 The Old Brewery
1889-1971 Town Hall, Parliament Square
1971- Station Road

CASTLETOWN
1845-1896 Military Barracks, Market Place
1890-1896 Union Hotel Yard, Arbory Street
1896-1898 The former Barracks
1898-1912 Alexandra Road,
1912-1965 Commissioners Yard, The Old Barracks
1965- Farrants Way

PORT ERIN
1897-1934 Commissioner's Yard, Station Road
1934-1939 Falcon's Nest Yard

PORT ST MARY
1907-1939 Hosebox at Police Station
1921-1939 Harper's Yard

ONCHAN
1911-1938 Coupe's Stables, Queens Road
1938-1940 Commissioners Yard, School Road

LAXEY
1920-1943 Commissioner's Office, New Road
1943- Mines Road

KIRK MICHAEL
1931-1940 Commissioners Store, Main Road
1940-1942 Kelly's Yard, Main Road
1942-1942 Quayle's Garage, Main Road
1942-1979 Mitre Hotel Car Park
1979- Station Road

FOXDALE
1942- Main Road, Upper Foxdale

ANDREAS
1942- Andreas Village

BALLASALLA
1942- Crossag Road, Ballasalla

RUSHEN
1939-1958 Falcon's Nest Yard, Port Erin
1942-1955 Commissioners Yard, Athol St, Port St Mary
1958- Droghadfayle Road, Port Erin

ii. LIST OF CAPTAINS OR CHIEF OFFICERS

DOUGLAS
1860-1867 Mr C Craine
1867-1871 Mr J Cartwright
1871-1890 Mr W Kewley
1890-1903 Mr R O'Hara
1903-1921 Mr W Pickett (Captain)
1903-1916 Mr R O'Hara (Superintendent)
1921-1929 MrS J Caugherty (Captain)
1921-1929 Mr W Pickett (Superintendent)
1929-1935 Mr A J O'Hara (Captain)
1929-1935 Mr S J Caugherty (Superintendent)
1935 BRIGADE STRUCTURE REVISED
1935-1945 Mr S A Caugherty
1945-1950 Mr A J O'Hara
1950-1965 Mr F Courtie
TRANSFERRED TO IoM FIRE SERVICE

PEEL
1885-1895 Mr W Kermode
1895-1901 Mr H Quayle
1901-1933 Mr T E Watterson
1933-1942 Mr E Cowell
1942-1946 Mr R H Kneen
1946-1955 Mr W H Watterson
1955-1960 Mr J Bell
TRANSFERRED TO IoM FIRE SERVICE

RAMSEY
1887-1900 MR W Boyde (Superintendant)
1887-1900 Mr A Wall (Captain)
1900-1918 Mr W Boyde
1918-1921 Police Inspector King
1921-1928 Police Inspector Fayle
1928-1942 Mr J Smith
1942-1945 Mr J W Sayle
1945-1960 Mr J R Brooke
TRANSFERRED TO IoM FIRE SERVICE

CASTLETOWN
1896-1921 Mr J Cubbon
1921-1928 Mr J Kneale
1928-1942 Mr T Corkill
1942-1944 Mr J W Oates
1944-1960 Mr F L Kennaugh
TRANSFERRED TO IoM FIRE SERVICE

PORT ERIN
1897-1915 Mr Wm Harrison (Escape Minder)
1915-1927 Mr Wm Harrison (Captain)
1927-1933 PC. A Corris
1933-1937 PC J Lace
1937-1939 PC A Cowin
AMALGAMATED WITH PORT ST MARY AS THE RUSHEN JOINT FIRE PROTECTION BOARD

PORT ST MARY
1907-1912 P Sgt E.H.Corkill (Hose Minder)
1912-1912 P Sgt Wm Fargher (Hose Minder)
-1936 Mr J Cubbon (Superintendent)
1936-1939 Mr J Crebbin
AMALGAMATED WITH PORT ERIN AS THE RUSHEN JOINT FIRE PROTECTION BOARD

RUSHEN JOINT FIRE PROTECTION BOARD
1939-1941 PC A Cowin
1941-1947 Mr J R Costain
1947-1950 Mr J Hyslop
RECONSTITUTED AS THE RUSHEN FIRE AUTHORITY

RUSHEN FIRE AUTHORITY
1950-1960 Mr J Hyslop
TRANSFERED TO THE IoM FIRE SERVICE

ONCHAN
1911- Mr J T Skillicorn
-1940 Mr E Quiggin
DISBANDED UNDER THE TERMS OF
THE 1940 (FIRES) ACT

LAXEY
1920-1930 Mr F B Holroyed
1930-1947 Mr D Williamson
1947-1960 Mr W J Bridson (Sen)
TRANSFERED TO IoM FIRE SERVICE

KIRK MICHAEL
1931-1941 Mr F W Cowin
1941-1951 PCG WA Kinrade
1951-1952 PCP Moyer
1952-1960 Mr G E Creer
TRANSFERRED TO IoM FIRE SERVICES

ISLE OF MAN FIRE SERVICE

CHIEF FIRE STAFF OFFICERS
1941-1950 Mr C A P Ellis
1951-1961 Mr S J Mayall
1961-1962 Mr F Courtie (acting)
1962-1974 Mr C Pearson
1974- Mr J Hinnigan

DEPUTY CHIEF OFFICERS
1965-1966 Mr F Courtie
1966-1976 Mr S Skinner
1976-1990 Mr R J I Hopkins
1990- Mr W G Cain

OFFICERS IN CHARGE OF STATIONS

DOUGLAS STATION
1965-1965 Mr H B Kenna
1965-1966 Mr R S Skinner
1966-1981 Mr M M Ventre
1981-1990 Mr W G Cain
1990- Mr A D Christian

PEEL STATION
1960-1970 Mr J Bell
1970-1974 Mr J Killey
1974- Mr L Halsall

RAMSEY STATION
1960-1968 Mr J R Brooke
1968-1974 Mr G Foulis
1974-1990 Mr P B Quayle
1990- Mr G D Foulis

CASTLETOWN STATION
1960-1968 Mr F L Kennaugh
1968-1975 Mr A Kelly
1975-1988 Mr A L Sayle
1988- Mr T E Craine

RUSHEN STATION
1960-1968 Mr J Hyslop
1968-1971 Mr D T Quine
1971-1984 Mr A J Corkish
1984-1986 Mr B T Peyton
1986- Mr N T Gandy

LAXEY STATION
1960-1974 Mr W J Bridson (Sen)
1974-1982 Mr W J Bridson (Jun)
1982- Mr J Boyde

KIRK MICHAEL STATION
1960-1964 Mr G E Creer
1964-1965 Mr L Lowe (Acting)
1965-1967 Mr L Lowe
1967-1974 Mr D Collins
1974-1977 Mr J Lowe
1977-1981 Mr R Telford
1981-1990 Mr L E Teare
1990- Mr D Mayne

RONALDSWAY AIRPORT FIRE SERVICE
1946-1970 Mr A Corlett
1970-1978 Mr R W C Corkish
1978-1986 Mr L Kinrade
1986- Mr D Young

iii. LIST OF FIRE APPLIANCES

DOUGLAS (SUN FIRE OFFICE)
Manual Pump 1803-1848
Manual Pump 1803-

DOUGLAS TOWN COMMISSIONERS
Manual Pump "Grampus" McGhie,
Lewthwaite & Teare 1848-1884
Ladder Cart
Reel Cart Shand Mason & Co 1875-
50ft "Clayton" Wheeled Escape 1877-
Manual Pump "Douglas" Wm Rose & Co.
1884-
Reel Cart 1887-
45ft "Kingston" Wheeled Escape Wm
Rose & Co 1895-
36ft "Curricle" Wheeled Escape Wm Rose
& Co. 1895-

DOUGLAS CORPORATION
Steam Pump "Raglan" Merryweather &
Sons 1909-
65 HP Pump Escape Leyland MN 1233
1920-1948
50ft "Bayley" Wheeled Escape
14 HP Motor Tender Bean MN 6117
1929-1941 (sold to Castletown Commissioners)
"Hatfield" trailer pump Merryweather
1935-
100ft turntable ladder Dorman/
Merryweather MAN 875 1936-1962
Major pump Albion/Merryweather MAN
876 1936-
Motor tender Fordson EMN 823 1941-1965
(transferred to LGB 1965)
All auxilliary towing vehicles had light
trailer pumps which were retained by fire
service
Auxiliary towing vehicle Austin FMN 237
1942-1946 (sold to J Curtis Ltd.)
Auxiliary towing vehicle Austin FMN 238
1942-1955 (transferred to Rushen Fire
Authority)
Auxiliary towing vehicle Austin FMN 248
1942-1946 (sold to Douglas Holiday
Camp)

Auxiliary towing vehicle Austin FMN 280
1942-1946 (sold to I O M Dairies)
Major pump/escape Merryweather NMN
50 1951-1965 (transferred to LGB 1965)
Auxiliary towing vehicle Austin FMN 267
1955-1962 (sold to Davies Garage)
Pump water tender F28 Dennis 5531 MN
1962-1965 (transferred to LGB 1965)
100ft turntable ladder AEC/
Merryweather 5724 MN 1962-1965
(transferred to LGB 1965)
Personnel carrier Commer 6002 MN 1962-
1965 (transferred to LGB 1965)

RAMSEY (SUN FIRE OFFICE)
Manual pump 1803-1808
(transferred to Douglas)

RAMSEY TOWN COMMISSIONERS
Handcart Wm Rose & Co 1887-
Manual pump 1888-
60ft wheeled escape Shand Mason & Co
1896- (preserved by IoM Fire Service)
30HP Motor pump "Richdale"
Merryweather MN 5695 1928-1942
24HP Motor tender Morris/Merryweather
EMN 106 1939-1954 (sold to Civil Defence
Commission)
"Hatfield" No 2 trailer pump
Merryweather
25HP pump escape Merryweather EMN
204 1940-1955 (sold to Laxey Commissioners)
Auxiliary towing vehicle Austin FMN 284
1942-1960 (transferred to LGB 1960)
Pump water tender F8 Dennis TMN 424
1955-1960 (transferred to LGB 1960)

CASTLETOWN BARRACKS
Manual pump J Stone & Co 1845-1896
(sold to Castletown Commissioners)

CASTLETOWN COMMISSIONERS
Hand Fire Cart J Morris & Co 1890-
Manual pump J Stone & Co 1896-1955
(given to the Manx Museum)
14HP Motor tender Bean MN 6117
1941-1942 (sold to Kirk Michael
Commissioners)

Auxiliary towing vehicle Austin FMN 259 1942-1953 (transferred to Civil Defence Commission)

Auxiliary towing vehicle Austin FMN 451 1943-1946 (transferred to IoM Government)

Pump water tender F8 Dennis PMN 72 1953-1960 (transferred to LGB 1960)

PEEL TOWN COMMISSIONERS

Hand fire cart Wm Rose & Co 1885-1941

Manual pump Shand Mason & Co 1921-

Motor tender Commer/Merryweather EMN 983 1941-1953

(sold to Civil Defence Commission)

"Hatfield" trailer pump Merryweather

Auxiliary towing vehicle Austin FMN 404 1942-1946 (transferred to Kirk Michael Commissioners)

Pump water tender F8 Dennis PMN 71 1953-1960 (transferred to LGB 1960)

PORT ERIN VILLAGE COMMISSIONERS

60ft wheeled escape Wm Rose & Co 1897-

45ft extending ladder and implement van H Simmis & Co 1914-

RUSHEN JOINT FIRE PROTECTION BOARD (Rushen Fire Authority)

50ft Escape carrier Morris/Merryweather DMN 890 1939-1960 and Beresford light trailer pump (transferred to LGB 1960)

Auxiliary towing vehicle Austin FMN 267 1942-1955 (sold to Douglas Corporation)

Auxiliary towing vehicle Austin FMN 238 1955-1956 (sold to Michael Commissioners)

Personnel carrier/hose carrier Austin A30 1955-

4 x 4 light pump Austin Gypsy 601 MN 1959-1960 (transferred to LGB 1960)

LAXEY VILLAGE COMMISSIONERS

Hand fire cart J Blakeborough & Sons Ltd. 1920 (preserved by the I O M Fire Service)

Motor Tender Dodge BMN 207 1940-1941 (sold to the I O M Harbour Board)

Auxiliary towing vehicle Austin FMN 249 1942-1955 (transferred to Civil Defence Commission)

Major pump Merryweather EMN 204 1955-1960 (transferred to LGB 1960)

KIRK MICHAEL VILLAGE COMMISSIONERS

Hand fire cart

14 HP motor tender Bean MN 6117 1942-1946

Auxiliary towing vehicle Austin FMN 404 1946-1956 (transferred to Civil Defence Commission)

Auxiliary towing vehicle Austin FMN 238 1956-1960 (transferred to LGB 1960)

ISLE OF MAN GOVERNMENT

(Salvage Division Government Office)

Van 12HP Morris DMN 925 1940-1946

Saloon Car 8HP Morris FMN 493 1943-1945

Auxiliary towing vehicle Austin FMN 451 1943-1955 (transferred to Civil Defence Commission)

Government Office (transport for Chief Fire Staff Officer)

Saloon car 8HP Ford FMN 196 1942-1948

HARBOUR BOARD

Motor tender Dodge BMN 207 1941-1947

CIVIL DEFENCE COMMISSION

Motor Tender Commer EMN 983 1953-1965 (sold to the Manx Motor Museum)

Auxiliary towing vehicle Austin FMN 259 1953-

Motor tender Morris EMN 106 1954-1967 (loaned to King William's College)

Major pump Austin GMN 882 1955-1967

Auxiliary towing vehicle Austin FMN 249 1955-1973

Auxiliary towing vehicle Austin FMN 451 1955-1968

Auxiliary towing vehicle Austin FMN 404 1956-1970

Major pump Bedford Green Goddess 311 HMN 1967-1974

Major pump Bedford Green Goddess 876 KMN 1968-1974 (loaned to King William's College)

Major pump Bedford Green Goddess 878 KMN 1968-1968 (transferred to Fire Service)

Major pump Bedford Green Goddess 877 KMN 1968-1974

LOCAL GOVERNMENT BOARD (ISLE OF MAN FIRE SERVICE)

DOUGLAS STATION (FIRE 1)

Major pump escape Merryweather/AEC NMN 50 1965-1968

Motor tender Fordson EMN 823 1965-1968

Pump water tender Dennis F28 5531 MN 1965-1971 (allocated to Castletown)

100ft turntable ladder AEC/Merryweather 5724 MN 1965-1988

Personnel carrier Commer 6002 MN 1965-1968

Emergency tender Land Rover 999 KMN 1968-1979

Pump escape Dennis F35 999 CMN 1968-1988

Pump water tender Dennis F46A 999 WMN 1971

Major pump/command vehicle Bedford Green Goddess 311 HMN 1974197

Hydraulic platform ERF/Simon NMN 999 1975-

General purpose van Leyland Sherpa MAN 103T 1977-1990

Emergency tender Ford HMN 999 1979-

Foam tender/hose carrier Dennis F8 PMN 72 1980-1984

Jetmaster trailer mounted foam monitor

Water tender ladder Dennis RS61 KMN 999 1980-

4 x 4 tender Austin Gypsy 442 LMN 1981-1990

Foam tender/hose carrier Dennis F28 5531 MN 1984-1988

Foam tender/hose carrier Volvo FL10/Nova Scotia MAN 999B 1988-

30m turntable ladder Volvo FL6/Metz MAN 999U 1988-

Water tender ladder Volvo FL6/Fulton Wylie MAN 999P 1990-

4 x 4 water tender ladder Mercedes/Carmichael BMN 999U 1990-

4 x 4 general purpose van Nissan BMN

999W 1990-

LAXEY STATION (FIRE 2)

Major pump Merryweather EMN 204 1960-1961 (converted and allocated to Michael)

Pump water tender Dennis F28 1817 MN 1960-1981

4 x 4 light pump Austin Gypsy 601 MN 1981-1987

Pump water tender Dennis DS OMN 999 1981-

4 x 4 water tender ladder Unimog/Fulton Wylie BMN 999A 1987-1990 (transferred to Rushen)

4 x 4 pump water tender Land Rover 999 LMN 1990-

RAMSEY STATION (FIRE 3)

Auxiliary towing vehicle Austin FMN 284 1960-1962

Pump water tender Dennis F8 TMN 424 1960-1979

Escape carrier Morris DMN 890 1962-1967

Pump escape Dennis F38 999 GMN 1967-

Emergency tender Leyland Sherpa MAN 579X 1978-

Pump water tender Dennis R61 999 UMN 1979-

4 x 4 pump water tender Land Rover FMN 999 1978-1990 (transferred to reserve)

6 x 6 water tender ladder Pinzgauer/Saxon BMN 999R 1990-

KIRK MICHAEL STATION (FIRE 4)

Auxiliary towing vehicle Austin FMN 238 1960-1961

Pump water tender Merryweather EMN 204 1961-1963

4 x 4 pump water tender Land Rover FMN 999 1963-1978 (transferred to Ramsey)

4 x 4 light pump Austin Gypsy 601 MN 1968-1981 (transferred to Laxey)

Pump water tender Dennis R61 PMN 999 1978-

4 x 4 pump water tender Land Rover/Pilcher Green NMN 999 1981-

PEEL STATION (FIRE 5)

Pump water tender Dennis F8 PMN 71 1960-1975

4 x 4 pump water tender Land Rover EMN 999 1964-1989

Pump water tender ERF WMN 999 1975-1981 (converted to pump escape) 1981-

6 x 6 water tender ladder Pinzgauer/ Saxon BMN 999L 1989-

RUSHEN STATION (FIRE 6)

Escape carrier Morris DMN 890 1960-1962 (transferred to Ramsey)

Light pump Austin Gypsy 601 MN 1960-1968 (transferred to Kirk Michael)

Pump escape Dennis F28 5716 MN 1962-1983

4 x 4 pump water tender Land Rover 999 LMN 1968-1990 (transferred to Laxey)

Pump escape Dennis DS TMN 999 1983-

4 x 4 water tender ladder Unimog/Fulton Wylie BMN 999A 1990-

CASTLETOWN STATION (FIRE 7)

Pump water tender Dennis F8 PMN 72 1960-1980 (transferred to Douglas)

Major pump Bedford Green Goddess 878 KMN 1968-1977 (transferred to Douglas)

Pump water tender ERF 999 MMN 1977-

Pump water tender Dennis F28 5531 MN 1980-1984 (transferred to Douglas)

4 x 4 tender Austin Gypsy 441 LMN 1981-

Pump water ladder Dennis DS 999 PMN 1984-

RONALDSWAY AIRFIELD

Crash tender 12HP Morris Van 1935-1940

RONALDSWAY (HMS URLEY)

Major pump Austin RN 40307 1940-1946

Crash tender Fordson WOT 1 RN 29686 1940-1946

Crash tender Crossley RN 37214 1940-1946

These appliances were registered by the Ministry of Civil Aviation on 28th August 1946 and subsequently purchased by the Isle of Man Airports Board, being registered in their ownership on 26th June 1951

RONALDSWAY (AIRPORT FIRE SERVICE)

Major pump Leyland MN 1233 1948-1951

Major pump Austin GMN 882 1951-1955 (sold to Civil Defence Commission)

Crash tender Fordson WOT 1 GMN 888 1951-1969

Crash tender Crossley GMN 889 1951-1967

Foam tender Thornycroft/Pyrene TMN 760 1955-1979

Foam tender Ford Thames Trader XMN 917 1959-1978

Personnel rescue Austin Gypsy 444 LMN 1959-1984

CO2 tender Austin 1819 MN 1960-1979 (sold to Thermo Skyships, Jurby)

Water tender/domestic Bedford/Angus 621 BMN 1965-1990

Foam tender Fire 3 Thornycroft Nubian MK 2 MN 4359 1973-

Rapid intervention vehicle Fire 1 Range Rover/Carmichael B54 MAN 1979-

Foam tender Fire 2 Jet Ranger 2000/ Carmichael E526 MAN 1979-

Personnel rescue/IRB Series 2A Land Rover MAN 381L 1984-1987

Personnel rescue/IRB Toyota Hilux J119 MAN 1987-1989

Personnel rescue/IRB Fire 5 Daihatsu Fourtrax BMN 36P 1989-

Foam tender Fire 4 Simon Saro Defender BMN 731W 1990-

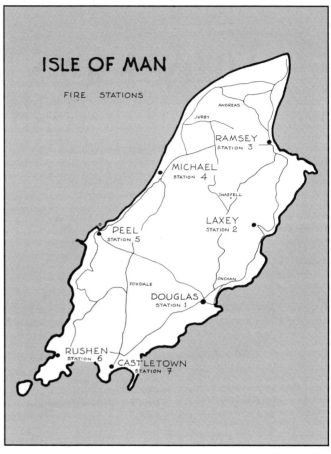

Appendix iv — Map showing the location of the principal towns and villages of the Isle of Man and current fire-fighting provision.

NO ONE KNOWS THE ROPES BETTER THAN WE DO.

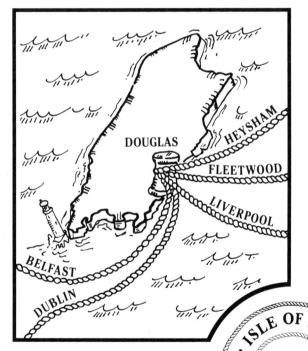

With five routes and over a thousand sailings throughout the year, we've got the Isle of Man covered.

FERRY SERVICES

Our two refurbished ships, King Orry and Lady of Mann present the highest standards of comfort on the Irish Sea and will transport you, your family and your car in true style, at unbeatable prices.

MAGIC HOLIDAYS

Inclusive Magic Holidays and Short Breaks, represent terrific value for money, with packages to suit everyone.

FREIGHT SERVICES

No other method of freight forwarding can bridge the gap so speedily, efficiently and effectively as our regular overnight Ro-Ro freight service out of Heysham. Winter or Summer, Business or Pleasure, we've got the connections to get you going.
For details, telephone: **(Ferry Services) 0624 661661, (Magic Holidays) 0624 673399, (Freight Services) 0624 626503.**

ISLE OF MAN · STEAM PACKET COMPANY